FOR KING & EMPIRE

THE CANADIANS AT VIMY, April 1917

ARLEUX, April 28th, 1917
FRESNOY, May 3rd, 1917

A Social History and Battlefield Tour

by N. M. Christie

FOR KING & EMPIRE; VOLUME III
REVISED EDITION

CEF BOOKS
2002

The publisher would like to thank Mr. Gary Roncetti for his contributions to this book.

National Library of Canada Cataloguing in Publication

Christie, N. M.
     The Canadian at Vimy, April 1917/Norm Christie. --Rev. ed.

(For King & Empire ; v. 3)
ISBN 1-896979-33-5

1. Vimy Ridge, Battle of, 1917. 2. Canada. Canadian Army--History--World War, 1914-1918. 3. World War, 1914-1918--Battlefield--France--Vimy--Tours. I. Title. II. Series: Christie, N. M. . For King & Empire ; v. 3.
D545.V5C48 2002   940.4'31   C2002-904462-6

Published by: CEF BOOKS
                      P.O. Box 40083
                      Ottawa, Ontario, K1V 0W8
                      1-613-823-7000

The "For King & Empire" Series

Volume I:	The Canadians at Ypres, 22nd-26th April 1915
Volume II:	The Canadians on the Somme, September-November 1916
Volume III:	The Canadians at Vimy, April 1917
Volume IV:	The Canadians at Passchendaele, October-November 1917
Volume V:	The Canadians at Arras, August-September 1918
Volume VI:	The Canadians at Cambrai, September-October 1918
Volume VII:	The Canadians at Amiens, August 1918
Volume VIII	The Canadians at Mount Sorrel, June 1916

Also from CEF BOOKS:
Ghosts Have Warm Hands by Will R. Bird, MM
Letters of Agar Adamson   Edited by N.M. Christie
The Journal of Private Fraser   Edited by Dr. R.H. Roy
For Freedom and Honour?   by A. B. Godefroy

Front Cover: The Vimy Memorial, France. The Spirit of Canada weeps for her fallen sons.

Back cover: Corporal Henry Pegram, 72nd Seaforth Highlanders, only son of Kate Pegram of Vancouver, killed at Vimy Ridge, April 9th, 1917.

Vimy Ridge

Tread softly here! Go reverently and slow!
Yea, let your soul go down upon its knees,
And with bowed head, and heart abased, strive hard
To grasp the future gain in this sore loss!
For not one fool of this dank sod but drank
Its surfeit of the blood of gallant men,
Who, for their faith, their hope, - for Life and Liberty,
Here made the sacrifice, - here gave their lives,
And gave right willingly - for you and me.

From this vast altar-pile the souls of men
Sped up to God in countless multitudes;
On this grim cratered ridge they gave their all,
And, giving, won
The Peace of Heaven and Immortality.
Our hearts go out to them in boundless gratitude;
If ours - then God's; for His vast charity
All sees, all knows, all comprehends - save bounds.
He has repaid the sacrifice; - and we - - ?
God help us if we fail to pay our debt
In fullest and all unstintingly!

John Oxenham
1852-1941

TABLE OF CONTENTS

INTRODUCTION
THE BATTLE OF VIMY RIDGE, April 1917

The capture of Vimy Ridge in April 1917 is considered one of the major building blocks of Canada. It is one of the few battles of the First World War which has a place in Canada's consciousness.

On April 9th, 1917, for the first time in the war, all four Canadian Infantry Divisions attacked side by side. Their capture of the "impregnable" German bastion of Vimy Ridge brought instantaneous response. For the first time in the war, the Allies had won something tangible. The French, who suffered heavy losses during a failed attempt to take the Ridge in 1915, were ecstatic. With Vimy in Canadian hands, the "martyred" French city of Arras was free from the German threat.

The Canadians' performance was celebrated throughout the Allied countries. But the cost for Canada was heavy. More than 3,600 Canadian soldiers were killed between April 9th and 12th. Over the entire month of April, 5,008 Canadians died. It was the worst month of the war. But the victory seemed worth the cost.

The capture of Vimy Ridge in 1917 was as much a propaganda victory as a military one. The year had started with such promise, but quickly turned into the Allies' bleakest year and finally petered out dismally in the morass of Passchendaele.

And so the victories of the Canadians at Vimy and Arleux in April, Fresnoy in May, Hill 70 in August and Passchendaele in November assumed significant proportions well beyond the realities of the gains. The reputation of the Canadian Corps as the most efficient fighting machine and of Canada itself was sealed. Canada had earned a voice of its own.

The efficiency achieved by the Canadian Corps continued to evolve. In 1918, the Canadians spearheaded the victory of the last hundred days of the war with stunning successes at Amiens, Arras and Cambrai.

But the legacy was born at Vimy Ridge. And today, the Canadian National Memorial to the Great War stands astride Hill 145. It is the most impressive memorial of the First World War and is surrounded by 250 hectares of dilapidated trenches, shell holes and mine craters. This Canadian Memorial Park, a piece of Canada in the heart of northern France, is the same as on that fateful Easter morning of 1917, without the trees and grass.

Still visible outside the park are the lonely abandoned 44th Battalion (Manitoba) Memorial near the Pimple, the 3rd Division Memorial in La Folie Wood and the 1st Division Memorial near Thélus. All these, the reconstructed trenches and tunnels within the park and the military cemeteries of the Great War easily remind the visitor of the battle. Vimy is the best preserved Canadian battlefield of the First World War.

My grandfather's memories of Vimy were always mingled with his pride in being Canadian. That legacy has passed on to me as it is part of what it means to be Canadian.

The legacy was even more clear to the sons of the men of Vimy. In a Second World War Canadian War Cemetery at Bayeux, Normandy lies the grave of Gunner John V. Mugford of the Royal Canadian Artillery. He was killed July 14th, 1944, near Caen. He was 21. His middle initial stands for Vimy.

The Commander of the Canadian forces that captured Vimy Ridge in April 1917: The late Lord Byng of Vimy (then Lt.-Gen. Sir Julian Byng; seated, center) in a contemporary group of Officers taken at the Canadian Corps headquarters.

Getting There

This guide recommends Arras as the centre of operations for visiting the Vimy battlefields, which are 10 km north of the city. Arras is located in the Pas-de-Calais and is easily accessible from Paris (170 km) and Brussels (120 km). From London, it is a two-hour drive to Dover, a 75 minute ferry ride to Calais, and a 45 minute drive from Calais. The opening of the Channel Tunnel has made a direct rail link from London to Lille, France, which is 45 minutes from Arras. Check with the Tourist Board for details. Rental cars are available in any of the above-mentioned cities and tourist offices can supply routes and details of hotels.

In Arras very little English is spoken so brush up on your French before you leave. Most stores close between noon and 2 p.m., always be sure to get all your film and other necessities before lunch!

The Euro has replaced the French (and Belgian) Franc. The current exchange rate for Euros roughly 1.50 Canadian dollar per Euro (2002). Credit cards, such as VISA (Carte Bleu) or MasterCard are accepted, but please check with the hotel where you are staying. Always visit the Tourism Office to obtain information on accommodation and events of interest.

Theft is a real problem in France and in particular breaking into cars. The local thieves will drill the lock, take what they want and be gone in seconds. Do not leave anything in plain view in your car and try to leave your vehicle within sight if possible. You have been warned.

What To Bring

Weather is very changeable in this part of Europe. Days can start sunny and change quickly to rain, hail or even a sprinkling of snow. Above all, be prepared for wet weather. For example, the average temperature in Belgium in July varies from 12 to 24°C.

Other than the obvious, a passport, traveller's checks and appropriate clothing, bring the following to ensure a successful trip:

-a bottle opener and cork screw
-binoculars
-a camera (with 400 ASA film)
-a compass
-rubber boots
-National Geographic Institute (IGN) maps 1:25,000, 2406 Arras East and 2506 Arras West. They are available in the many stores in Arras.
-Michelin map No.51 (preferably the Commonwealth War Graves Commission overprint, showing all the cemeteries, available at the CWGC Office at Beaurains)
-reference books (do your research before departure)
-a journal to record the details of your visit, because you will forget.

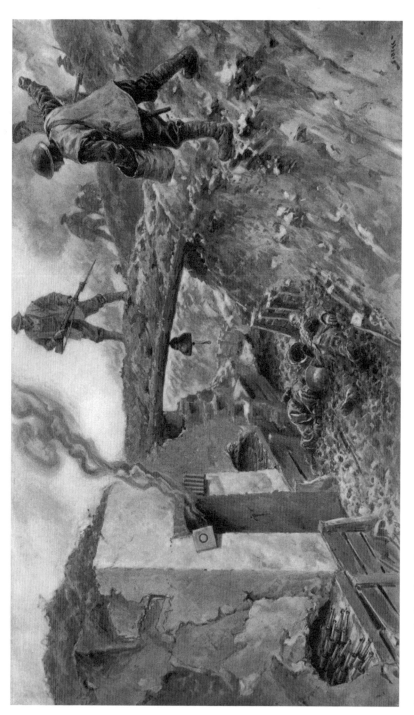

Preventing attacks from behind on our advancing troops: one man (right) bombing a German dug-out to force out the occupants, while another stands ready to compel surrender.

ABOUT ARRAS

Arras is the capital of the Artois region of northern France. Historically it has been the scene of many wars and the objective of many invading armies. This was the case during the First World War when the Germans briefly overran the city in 1914, and were driven out after a brief occupation. Arras was never far from the frontline and throughout the next four years was constantly bombarded. Its beautiful architecture was badly damaged by the shell-fire and it gained the reputation of being a "martyred " place, much like Ypres. Virtually every Canadian who fought in the war knew Arras. It is in many ways, one of those soulful cities that was deeply imbued in the consciousness of the Great War generation.

It is the perfect place to visit the Vimy battlefields, only 7 km away. For those also making the pilgrimage to the other Canadian battlefields of the First World War, such as the Somme 1916, Arras 1918 or Cambrai 1918, it is the best place to set-up.

Of Roman origin, Arras was a stronghold in Julius Caesar's day. It was originally built on Baudimont Hill, east of the Crinchon Stream which runs through the town and called Atrebatum after a tribe which lived in the area, the Atrebates. Arras is a corruption of that name.

In the 5th century, during the reign of the Frankish king, Clovis I, Christianity was preached by Saint-Vaast, who created the diocese of Arras and was its first bishop. The most important abbey in the region was built in the 600s to honour the saint. A new town gradually emerged under the protection of this powerful monastery and eventually separated from the original construction by a continuous line of fortifications. By the 11th century, the two communities were quite independent of each other, each with its own form of government. The older Roman city on Baudimont Hill was the Cité of Arras and was under the jurisdiction of the bishop. The other, to the west, was the Ville proper and a dependency of the St. Vaast Abbey.

While the Ville grew steadily, the Cité gradually declined until the mid-18th century when it was incorporated in the Ville. Until Arras became part of the kingdom in France in the mid-17th century, the "Ville", as the capital of the County of Artois, successively belonged to the Counts of Flanders (850-1180), to the Counts of Artois (1180-1384), to the Dukes of Burgundy (1384-1492) and finally to the Kings of Spain (1492-1640).

The French kings often interfered in the affairs of Arras throughout this period. The town was besieged four times by the kings of France in the 9th and 10th centuries. In the 14th century, Arras was torn by popular sedition. Under the Dukes of Burgundy, and especially under Philippe-le-Bon, the town's world-renowned cloth and tapestry industries enjoyed a period of great prosperity. Its Arrazi tapestries became famous.

Arras is also infamous for imprisoning Joan of Arc during October and November 1430.

When Louis XI tried to claim Artois in 1477, the Cité of Arras promptly opened its gates to the Royal Army, but the Ville refused to surrender and was only conquered in 1479, after a long siege. Furious at the people's resistance, Louis XI exiled all the inhabitants and brought in the "Ligeriens." Arras became Spanish and its name was changed to Franchise. A few months later, the people of Arras were allowed to return to their homes, and in 1483, its ancient name, armorial bearings and laws were restored. (Just west of Arras are the battlefields of Crecy and Agincourt.)

The inhabitants of Arras resisted French domination for years following the incident with Louis XI. They opened their gates to the German and Burgundian troops of Austria in 1492, only to regret doing so when the Germans pillaged and rifled their valuables.

The Spanish-controlled city again came under the rule of the kings of France in the mid-17th century, when it fell after a long and bloody siege. The bombardments caused great damage to the abbey. A decade or so later, the town held out heroically against a Spanish invasion for 45 days.

Birth place of Augustin Robespierre, Arras was not spared during the Revolution. In 1793, Joseph Le Bon, sent there on a mission, organized the Terror. The guillotine was permanently erected in the Place de la Comédie. Travellers avoided Arras and the local merchants stopped doing business.

During the Great War, the Germans occupied Arras for only three days, September 6-9, 1914. But after their departure, the "Martyrdom of Arras" began. The Germans remained at the gates of the city until April 1917. Bombardment began October 6, 1914. Gunners fired ceaselessly on the military quarters and the two famous squares. The Hôtel de Ville, the Abbey of Saint Vaast and the Cathedral were burnt down, the belfry

Arras–Petite Place, May 1917

(PUBLIC ARCHIVES OF CANADA)

Arras–Hotel de Ville, May 1917

(PUBLIC ARCHIVES OF CANADA)

destroyed and by April 1917, Arras was completely in ruins. In March 1918, when the great German Offensive began, the bombardments broke out afresh, inhabitants were evacuated and by the end of August, the British drove the enemy out for good.

A visit to Arras should begin in the architecturally-unique Grand'Place, once an orchard belonging to the Abbey of Saint Vaast, and the Petite-Place. These squares have been bordered with gabled private houses and edged with stone columns and elliptical arches supporting vaulted galleries for hundreds of years.

Merchants once drew crowds of buyers to their stalls under the porticos of the squares and the famous tapestries of Arras were once made in the damp cellars under the galleries.

Bordering the west side of the Petite-Place is the Hôtel de Ville, above which rises the graceful silhouette of the belfry. Long the centre of town, the Petite-Place attracted the townspeople to public meetings, festivals and public executions.

Today, the tourist office is located at the Hôtel de Ville (03 21 51 26 95) and is open daily. From there, guided tours can be arranged of the underground tunnels beneath the town hall (35 minutes, year-round). First used as cellars, the tunnels often served as shelters for the population during invasions and for the soldiers of the First World War. You can also visit the belfry.

Two-hour tours of the town are also offered by guide-lecturers of the National Association for Historical Sites and Buildings daily in July and August at 3:00 p.m. and Wednesdays and Saturdays in June and September at 3:00 p.m. Reserve at the tourist office.

The Abbey of Saint-Vaast shelters the rich collections of the Museum, and is a masterpiece of classical religious architecture.

Note, most museums in France are open 10:00 a.m. to noon and 2:00 to 6:00 p.m. and closed on Tuesdays. Sunday and winter hours may be reduced. Abbey tel. 03 21 71 26 43.

Arras is famous for its "cobalt blue" porcelain, first produced in the late 18th century. It is available in most tourist shops in the town centre.

Accommodation is not a problem in Arras. You may want to check out the following hotels:

Astoria, 10 place Foch, 62000 Arras, tel. 03 21 71 08 14

Hôtel Ibis, place Viviani, 62000 Arras, tel. 03 21 23 61 61

Mercure Hôtel (3-star), 58 boulevard Carnot, 62000 Arras, tel.03 21 23 88 88

Hôtel Moderne, 1 boulevard Faidherbe, 62000 Arras, tel.03 21 23 39 57
Ostel des 3 Luppars, 47 Grand'Place, 62000 Arras, tel. 03 21 07 41 41
Hôtel de l'Univers, 5 place Croix Rouge, 62000 Arras, tel. 03 21 71 34 01

There are a wide variety of restaurants and cafés near the train station square and around the Grand and Petite Places.

BATTLEFIELD ARTIFACTS

Reminders of the Great War in the fields of France and Flanders are few and far between. Remnants of the trenches exist in the Memorial Parks at Vimy, Beaumont-Hamel and on a few French battlefields to the south toward Verdun. But, in general, the battlefields have returned to farmland and only the French, Commonwealth and German* cemeteries that scar the landscape reveal that Death once stalked these lands.

Nevertheless, as if not to be forgotten, the farmers' ploughing reveals an annual "harvest of steel" as evidence of the land's destructive history. Amazingly, after 80 years, numerous unexploded shells, grenades, bullets, buttons, pieces of equipment, fuses, and shrapnel balls by the thousands mount to the surface. After the ground is turned by the ploughs in late autumn, the winter rains wash away the surface to uncover the artifacts of battle. By February every year, thousands of relics of the Great War are sitting on top of the surface. You only need know where to look.**

Knowing where to look is in itself a bit of an art. You must determine where the main trenches ran through the use of trench maps or battlefield attack maps. On a secondary point, the state of the ground is also important as it is difficult to find anything in soil full of chalk or flint such as at The Pimple. Some chalk spoil is useful, however, in determining where the trenches ran. Even after eight decades, this spoil is evident and the ground itself is lower and softer.

Shrapnel balls are by far the most common find. Thousands are unearthed at the turn of a plough. (My five-year-old twin girls found 200 each in less than two hours on the Somme).

A word of caution is also necessary. You may find live ordnance such as shells or grenades. Do not touch these. While it is unlikely they will explode, that potential is still there. The use of a metal detector is usually regulated in France. Check with the local authorities if you wish to use one. And be careful.

Walking the battlefield is also an excellent way to become familiar with the battles and to gain a clear understanding of what occurred.

* There are also Portuguese, Russian and Italian cemeteries on the Western Front.
** Please remember these fields are private land and permission is required from the owner. Check with the local Mairie to find ownership.

COMPONENTS OF THE CANADIAN CORPS
Vimy Ridge, April 1917

1ST CANADIAN DIVISION

1ST INFANTRY BRIGADE	2ND INFANTRY BRIGADE	3RD INFANTRY BRIGADE
1ST BATTALION (WESTERN ONTARIO)	5TH BATTALION (SASKATCHEWAN)	13TH BATTALION (BLACK WATCH OF MONTREAL)
2ND BATTALION (EASTERN ONTARIO)	7TH BATTALION (BRITISH COLUMBIA)	14TH BATTALION (ROYAL MONTREAL REGIMENT)
3RD BATTALION (TORONTO REGIMENT)	8TH BATTALION (90TH RIFLES OF WINNIPEG)	15TH BATTALION (48TH HIGHLANDERS OF TORONTO)
4TH BATTALION (CENTRAL ONTARIO)	10TH BATTALION (ALBERTA)	16TH BATTALION (CANADIAN SCOTTISH)

2ND CANADIAN DIVISION

4TH INFANTRY BRIGADE	5TH INFANTRY BRIGADE	6TH INFANTRY BRIGADE
18TH BATTALION (WESTERN ONTARIO)	22ND BATTALION (CANADIEN-FRANÇAIS)	27TH BATTALION (CITY OF WINNIPEG)
19TH BATTALION (CENTRAL ONTARIO)	24TH BATTALION (VICTORIA RIFLES OF MONTREAL)	28TH BATTALION (SASKATCHEWAN)
20TH BATTALION (CENTRAL ONTARIO)	25TH BATTALION (NOVA SCOTIA)	29TH BATTALION (BRITISH COLUMBIA)
21ST BATTALION (EASTERN ONTARIO)	26TH BATTALION (NEW BRUNSWICK)	31ST BATTALION (ALBERTA)

3RD CANADIAN DIVISION

TH INFANTRY BRIGADE	8TH INFANTRY BRIGADE	9TH INFANTRY BRIGADE
ROYAL CANADIAN REGIMENT	1ST CANADIAN MOUNTED RIFLES (SASKATCHEWAN)	43RD BATTALION (CAMERON HIGHLANDERS OF WINNIPEG)
PRINCESS PATRICIA'S NADIAN LIGHT INFANTRY	2ND CANADIAN MOUNTED RIFLES (BRITISH COLUMBIA)	52ND BATTALION (NEW ONTARIO)
42ND BATTALION (BLACK WATCH OF MONTREAL)	4TH CANADIAN MOUNTED RIFLES (CENTRAL ONTARIO)	58TH BATTALION (CENTRAL ONTARIO)
49TH BATTALION (ALBERTA)	5TH CANADIAN MOUNTED RIFLES (QUEBEC)	60TH BATTALION (VICTORIA RIFLES OF MONTREAL)

4TH CANADIAN DIVISION

TH INFANTRY BRIGADE	11TH INFANTRY BRIGADE	12TH INFANTRY BRIDAGE
44TH BATTALION (MANITOBA)	54TH BATTALION (BRITISH COLUMBIA)	38TH BATTALION (EASTERN ONTARIO)
46TH BATTALION (SASKATCHEWAN)	75TH BATTALION (MISSISSAUGA HORSE)	72TH BATTALION (SEAFORTH HIGHLANDERS OF VANCOUVER)
47TH BATTALION (BRITISH COLUMBIA)	87TH BATTALION (GRENADIER GUARDS OF MONTREAL)	78TH BATTALION (WINNIPEG GRENADIERS)
50TH BATTALION (ALBERTA)	102ND BATTALION (NORTH BRITISH COLUMBIA)	73RD BATTALION (BLACK WATCH OF MONTREAL)

PIONEERS:
85TH (NOVA SCOTIA
HIGHLANDERS)

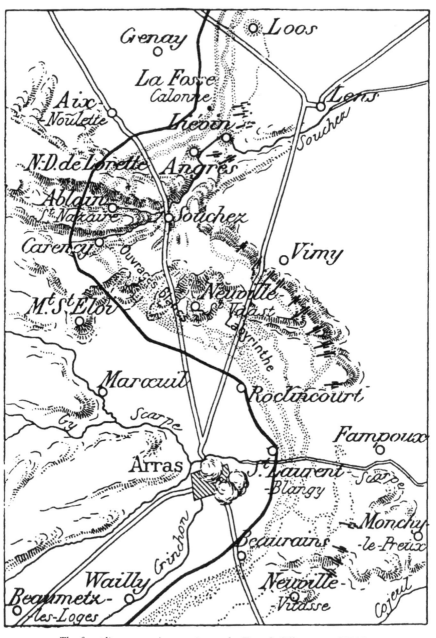

The front lines near Arras prior to the French Offensives of 1915.

THE BATTLE OF VIMY RIDGE

HISTORICAL OVERVIEW

The Vimy and Notre-Dame de Lorette Ridges at the northern approaches to Arras were the scenes of heavy fighting between the French and the Germans in 1915.

The ridges first came into prominence in September 1914 after the German Army was defeated at the Marne (near Paris). The Germans rapidly retreated northwards with the French and British armies in pursuit, the two sides attempting to outflank each other all the way to the Belgian coast. This "Race to the Sea" involved major and minor battles, including fighting north and east of Arras.

At the end of September, the French and Germans met head on. In successive attacks, the Germans captured Souchez and Neuville-St. Vaast, drove along the Notre-Dame de Lorette Ridge and came dangerously close to cutting off Arras from the north. The fighting continued until the end of 1914, when the front stabilized with the Germans in control of the eastern part of Notre-Dame de Lorette Ridge and the whole of Vimy Ridge.

With the Germans in such a powerful position, shelling at will, Arras was continuously in danger. In the s ring of 1915, the French high command decided to remove this threat. On May 9th, 1915, the 10th French Army attacked the German positions on a front extending from the Lorette Ridge to Neuville-St. Vaast.

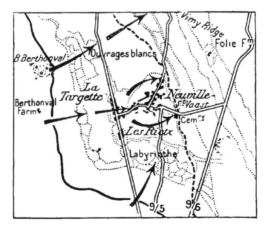

French attacks on Neuville-St. Vaast and the Labyrinthe May-June 1915.

At first, it was extremely successful. Moroccan troops smashed through the German positions between Neuville-St. Vaast and Souchez and reached the summit of Vimy Ridge. On the left of the Moroccans, the French 77th Division likewise broke through. Elsewhere, success was limited, and heavy fighting followed along the line of the attack and especially in The Labyrinthe, a maze of German trenches south of Neuville-St. Vaast. Unfortunately, German counterattacks drove them off Vimy Ridge. Although the French had improved their positions, the Germans still controlled the heights.

Notre-Dame de Lorette Ridge fell finally at the end of May, and the villages of Souchez, Ablain-St. Nazaire and Carency to the south were recaptured. Fighting against fierce opposition, the French finally captured the village of Neuville-St. Vaast and The Labyrinthe positions south of the village. The offensive had pushed the Germans off the important Notre-Dame de Lorette Ridge but, overall, had not achieved expectations. On June 19th, they called it off. It had cost the French more than 100,000 casualties.

The bodies of the fallen lay scattered in No Man's Land, in trenches and in shell holes. The stench of decaying flesh filled the summer air.

As part of a larger offensive, the British and French renewed the attack in Artois on September 25th, 1915. The objectives were the German positions opposite Souchez and on Vimy Ridge. The French advanced up the ridge and, after three days, captured The Pimple overlooking the village of Givenchy. Further south, they captured La Folie Farm on Vimy Ridge.

The Germans were better prepared than in May. Their counterattacks drove back the French and severe fighting continued for a few weeks. At the end of September, the Germans remained firmly in place on the heights of Vimy Ridge. However, the French had established positions along the western slope of the ridge which would become essential to the success of the Canadian attack of April 1917.

The main offensives were over but Vimy was not quiet yet. The fighting went underground and throughout 1916 and 1917 mining warfare was a continuous threat to both sides. The large craters blown out of the earth are visible today throughout the Vimy Park.

In March 1916, at a time when the mining battle was not proceeding well, British troops relieved the French in the Vimy sector. Their efforts changed the balance in the underground war.

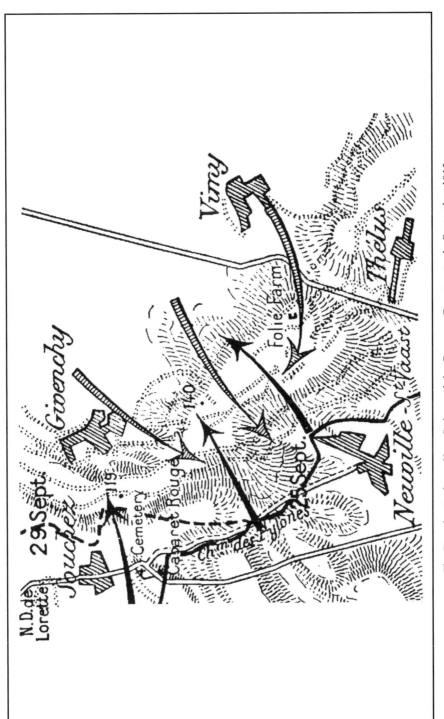

The French attacks on Vimy Ridge and the Germans Counterattacks September 1915.

On May 21st, 1916, the Germans launched a limited attack on the British forces between Broadmarsh Crater and Momber Crater opposite Hill 145. It was an attack designed to push back the British and to nullify their recent gains in the mining war. The British counterattacked and regained some lost territory but were unable to regain their original lines and lost 200 to 500 metres of valuable high ground. The French were none-to-pleased at the loss of that hard-won territory.

In October 1916, the Canadians arrived on the Vimy sector from the Somme battlefields in the south. By December, for the first time, all four Canadian Divisions were together.

The Allied plans for 1917 were ambitious. They planned a major two-prong attack on the German lines. The British would attack on a front from Croisilles, south of Arras, to Givenchy at the northern tip of Vimy Ridge. The French, a week later, would face the enemy at the Chemin-Des-Dames. The idea was to put an end to the German invasion and end the war.

The Canadians were charged with the responsibility of protecting the northern flank of the British attack. To accomplish this, they would have to capture Vimy Ridge. Unlike previous battles, particularly those haphazard attacks on the Somme, the Canadians rehearsed repeatedly. They probed the German lines and raided their trenches regularly to gain intelligence and to keep the Germans wary. Although these raids throughout the winter of 1916-1917 were successful, they resulted in the loss of many officers and men.*

On March 1st, 1917, the 4th Division launched the largest of all the Canadian raids against the German positions between The Pimple and Hill 145. It was a catastrophe! Six hundred and eighty-seven Canadians were lost, including the commanding officers of the 54th (Kootenay, British Columbia) and the 75th (Mississauga Horse) Battalions.** The 4th Division would pay for this loss of experienced men on April 9th.

The Canadian attack was to take place on a front of 6.1 km from the point where the trenches crossed the Arras-Lens road, north of Écurie, to Givenchy in the north.

---

* Not all Divisions in the Canadian Corps preferred this method. Arthur Currie's 1st Division, the Red Patch, believed the raids an unnecesary loss of experienced personnel and carried out the raids reluctantly.
** Lieutenant Colonel Arnold Kemball, 54th Battalion and Lieutenant Colonel Samuel Beckett, 75th Battalion. Both are buried in Villers Station Cemetery, Villers-aux-Bois.

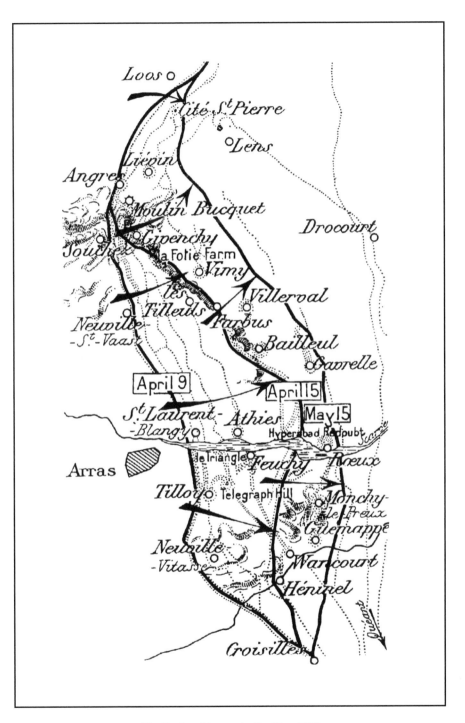

The Battle of Arras, April - May 1917.

The 1st Division would attack from their position west of the Arras-Lens road and capture the main German trenches in front of Thélus. For this they would employ six battalions in the main attack. From south to north, they would be the 5th (Saskatchewan), 7th (British Columbia), 10th (Alberta), 15th (48th Highlanders of Toronto), 14th (Royal Montreal Regiment) and 16th (Canadian Scottish) Battalions, attacking on a front of 1.8 km.

For the second phase, three battalions were to carry through the attack to capture German positions south of Thélus and push east of Thélus to Farbus. They were the 1st (Western Ontario), 3rd (Toronto Regiment) and 4th (Central Ontario) Battalions. To complete their objectives, they would have to advance 3.8 km. They had the furthest to go. However, in this region, the slope of the ridge is gentle and, unlike the 3rd and 4th Division sectors, had not been heavily fought over. It was to be a straightforward advance, if not an easy one.

North of the 1st Division, the 2nd Division would attack opposite Thélus along a 1.3 km front. Their objectives were similar to the 1st Division's, that is, to capture the main German trench positions in front of Thélus.

To do so, they would employ the 18th (Western Ontario), 19th (Central Ontario), 24th (Victoria Rifles of Montreal) and 26th (New Brunswick) Battalions. Once established in the main German trench, Zwischen Stellung, the 21st (Eastern Ontario) and 25th (Nova Scotia) Battalions would continue the attack toward Thélus. The 31st (Alberta) would be part of the final push to capture the village of Thélus, while the 28th (Saskatchewan) and 29th (British Columbia) would capture the trenches north of the village. Hill 135 was the responsibility of two attached British battalions, the 2nd Royal West Kents and the 2nd King's Own Scottish Borderers. The 29th and 27th (City of Winnipeg) Battalions would push on to Farbus and link up with the 1st Division.

The challenge to the 2nd Division was similar to that of the 1st. Here the distance was great but the defence clean and the slope gentle.

The 3rd Division was to attack on a front of 1.2 km opposite La Folie Wood. Their objective was to reach the eastern slope of Vimy Ridge, a distance of roughly one km. The terrain here had been cut up badly during the fighting of 1915. It was riven with shell holes, mine craters, old and new trenches and lent itself to defence. The 3rd Division would attack with six battalions.

South to north, they were the 1st Canadian Mounted Rifles (Saskatchewan), the 2nd CMR (British Columbia), the 4th CMR (Central Ontario), Royal Canadian Regiment, Princess Patricia's Canadian Light Infantry and the 42nd (Black Watch of Montreal) Battalion.

The 4th Division attacked from Broadmarsh Crater to Givenchy, a distance of 1.8 km. Their objective was Hill 145 and the eastern slopes of the ridge, a distance of 1.2 km. However short the distance, they were against the most heavily defended part of the ridge and their northern flank was open to enfilade fire from the strong German position of The Pimple. In addition, the ridge is very steep in this area and the severe fighting of 1915 had left the ground like a lunar landscape. The Germans would do everything to stop Hill 145 from falling into Canadian hands. From south to north, the attacking battalions of the 4th Division were the 54th and 102nd (both British Columbia), 87th (Grenadier Guards of Montreal) and 38th (Eastern Ontario). The 72nd (Seaforth Highlanders of Vancouver) and 73rd (Black Watch of Montreal) Battalions would protect the northern flank.

The 78th (Winnipeg Grenadiers) Battalion would carry the advance toward Givenchy village. The 4th Division held the 44th (Manitoba), 46th (Saskatchewan), 47th (British Columbia) and the 50th (Alberta) Battalions in reserve to capture The Pimple on the second day of the offensive.

The artillery preparation for the battle was immense. For two weeks, Canadian, British and South African artillery pounded the German positions. In the week preceding the attack, more than a million rounds of all sizes were fired. By the time of the advance on April 9th, they had obliterated many of the main German trenches and prevented supplies from reaching the German lines.

Besides the constant bombardment, the artillery had occupied itself sighting the placement of the German guns. Using sounding techniques, they would silence many German field pieces on the day of the attack. This effective counter battery fire would be a major factor in its success.

Once the battle started, the combined artillery had a tight schedule to keep German advanced positions subdued by a rolling barrage. The infantry, following the specific schedule, would advance. Undoubtedly, it was the artillery which was responsible for the victory at Vimy.

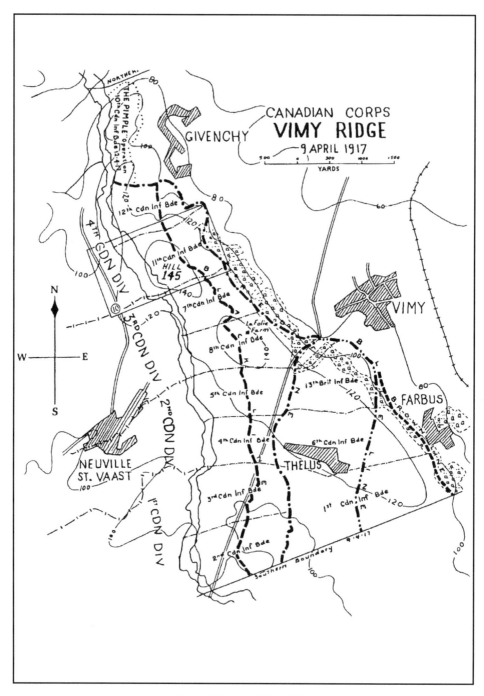

Vimy Ridge, April 9, 1917.

At 5:30 a.m. on Easter Monday, April 9th, 1917, in blowing sleet, the battle commenced.

The 1st Division's plan went well. The front line trenches fell quickly but resistance stiffened as they reached the second line. Each of the attacking battalions suffered 80 to 100 men killed. This meant one in eight of the advancing soldiers died.

Despite these heavy casualties, they pressed forward. Individual actions overcame difficult obstacles, particularly those caused by the large number of German machine gun nests. Private William Milne of the 16th Battalion, who was killed later in the attack, showed individual courage and initiative in eliminating German machine gun opposition and for his bravery was awarded the Victoria Cross. The second phase of the 1st Division's attack was equally successful and by the end of the day, they had achieved their objectives.

The 2nd Division's attack went according to plan and resistance was similar to that encountered by the 1st Division. Private Ellis Sifton of the 18th Battalion singlehandedly eliminated German opposition and was awarded the Victoria Cross, unfortunately, posthumously. Phase Two of the 2nd Division's advance on Thélus and the positions north of the village also went smoothly. By the end of the day, the 2nd Division had achieved all its objectives and suffered the least number of casualties.

Although the Germans were aware of the upcoming attack, they believed their positions were impregnable. The best example of their attitude is the 31st Battalion's capture of Thélus. They seized a large dugout complete with officers' bar, five uniformed waiters and a table laid for lunch! The German officers never had the opportunity to enjoy their meal. The dugout was only 1.3 km behind the front line.

The speed at which the defences had fallen shocked the Germans. However, the high end of the ridge was still in their hands.

The 3rd Division attack in the south also went well. The Canadian Mounted Rifle battalions overcame resistance, captured La Folie Farm and drove to the eastern edge of the wood. The northern attack started well, but the failure of the 4th Division resulted in many casualties. In spite of these problems, the three attacking battalions pushed through La Folie Wood and captured the positions south of Hill 145. German resistance was stiff and sniping, a particular German strength, resulted in many deaths. Although they had achieved the objectives, the situation was dangerous.

The southern attack by the 4th Division went well. The 102nd and 54th Battalions had pushed quickly across the German lines. The northern attack by the 73rd, 72nd and 38th Battalions had also advanced well and the battle was proceeding according to plan.

Meanwhile, the attack in the centre was a disaster. The 87th Battalion had failed to advance and, along with its supporting battalion, the 75th, was pinned down and being annihilated.

With the failure of the centre, the Germans turned their attention to the flanks, severely cutting up the 102nd, 54th, 38th and 72nd Battalions.

In the south, the 102nd and 54th Battalions managed to put up a defensive flank and continue their advance to the region south of Hill 145. The northern attack now faced more problems. The left flank was exposed to heavy machine gun fire from The Pimple. The 38th was suffering severely and was slowly being forced back. Captain Thain MacDowell and a small group of men of the 38th refused to yield their positions and kept up the Canadian flank. For MacDowell's bravery in these actions he was awarded a Victoria Cross. There can be no doubt his courageous action saved the northern flank and the men of the 72nd and 78th Battalions.

By the afternoon, groups of the 87th had started to move forward but were unable to capture Hill 145. This was a crucial position and, as long as it was in German hands, other Canadian gains were precarious. In a move of desperation, the 4th Division ordered the inexperienced 85th Battalion (Nova Scotia Highlanders) to capture Hill 145. Their miraculous capture of the Hill surprised the Germans.

German trenches east of the Hill were still causing trouble but, for the most part, the fighting of April 9th was over.

The losses for the 4th Division were shocking. One in four of the attacking soldiers was dead.

On April 10th, the 50th and 44th Battalions of the 4th Division attacked the remaining German positions on the ridge just east of Hill 145 and quickly captured them. Vimy Ridge was now in Canadian hands. None of the anticipated German counterattacks materialized. They had conceded the ridge.

The next Canadian attack was on April 12th. Again, battalions of the 4th Division — the 50th, 46th and 47th — attacked The Pimple. In a short and furious fight in blowing snow, The Pimple fell and the

Canadians pushed toward the village of Givenchy-en-Gohelle. A day later the Germans withdrew from Givenchy and pulled back onto the Douai Plain.

April 9th, 1917, had been a fantastic day all along the line for the Allies. They had achieved great success right across the Arras front. Although it was a great day for Canada, it had cost 3,600 Canadian lives.

In the following weeks, these successes turned into costly failures and the great promise of a breakthrough was buried in the bloody mud of Artois.

The share of the tanks taking Vimy Ridge: one (in foreground) crushing its way over a German machine-gun post, and firing its own "starboard" machine gun with deadly effect: another (in right background) flattening out the enemy's barbed wire.

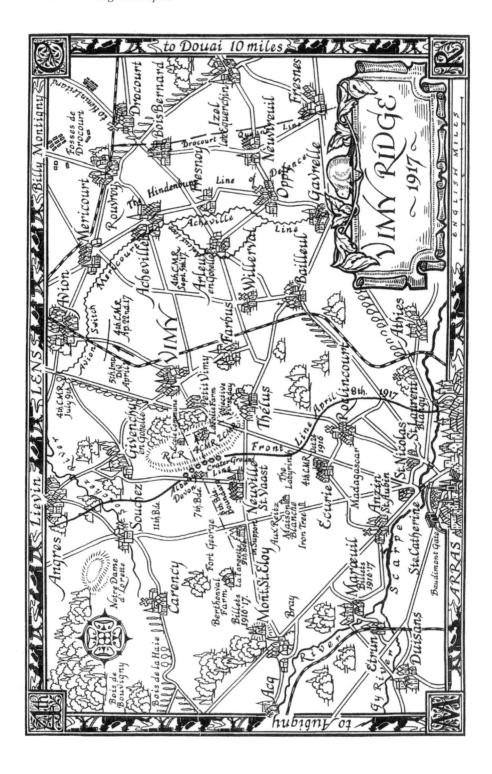

TOUR ITINERARY:
Duration 5-1/2 Hours

THE BATTLE OF VIMY RIDGE —
April 9th to 12th, 1917

Point 1: Notre-Dame de Lorette Ridge

Point 2: The Pimple, April 12th, 1917, 4th Division

Point 3: The flank of the 4th Division attack, April 9th, 1917

Point 4: Zouave Valley

Point 5: Broadmarsh Crater, 3rd and 4th Divisions

Point 6: Hill 145, The Vimy Memorial, 4th Division

Point 7: Lichfield Crater, the attack of the 2nd Division

Point 8: The attack of the 1st Division, Arras Road Military Cemetery

*Point 9: The follow-up attacks of the 1st and 2nd Divisions,
            April 9th, 1917, Thélus/Bois Carré*

Souchez, 1918

Neuville St. Vaast, 1919

THE BATTLE OF VIMY RIDGE

THE TOUR

The initial stage of this tour offers a general understanding of the significance of Vimy Ridge. The traveller will be exposed to the points of reference for orientation that can be viewed from almost any sector of the battlefield. The major landmarks are the ruins of Mont-St-Éloi Abbey 6.5 km west of Vimy Ridge, the Notre-Dame de Lorette Ridge northwest of Vimy Ridge and the city of Arras southwest of the ridge.

The tour begins in the Grand'Place of Arras. Leave the Grand'Place via the main road at the northeast corner of the square. Turn left onto the major road system and follow the signposts for Lille and the A1/A26 toll (péage) highway. Continue directly out of the city and head toward Béthune and Souchez. After 2.5 km, you come to a large traffic circle. The road to Béthune and Souchez is the D937. Cross the traffic circle, pass the D937 exit and follow the sign to Bruay-en-Artois. At the next main junction, turn right on the D341 and follow the signs to Mont-St-Éloi and Bruay-en-Artois. You will see the ruins of the abbey and a large multicolored water tower on your right. Follow the D341 for five km to Mont-St-Éloi. Turn right, onto the road that leads to the ruins, drive up the rise and stop at the abbey ruins.

The trees surrounding the ruins block the view of Vimy Ridge. However, the ruins themselves are quite interesting and are visible from virtually every point in this tour. Canadian troops held their reserves, established headquarters and stocked supplies at Mont-St-Éloi and in the hamlet of Ecoivres for two years.

Return to your car and continue east. The road turns sharply to the right and, after 1.6 km, meets the D49 to La Targette, and Neuville-St. Vaast. From here, Arras is clearly visible. To the east, you will see the cutting in the forest and the twin pylons of the Vimy Memorial. This road was a major communications link to the Canadian front lines at Vimy.

Turn left for La Targette. You reach La Targette after 2.5 km. Turn left on the D937 to Souchez.* Continue along the D937 to Souchez. The humpbacked ridge of Vimy, two km distant, and the Canadian monument on Hill 145, the highest point on the ridge, are clearly visible on your right.

After 1.3 km, you pass a Czechoslovak cemetery (for both World Wars) on your left and a memorial to Polish soldiers killed near here in 1915 on your right. Off to the right, you will see the two Canadian cemeteries among the trees of Vimy Park. Directly ahead is the Notre-Dame de Lorette French national cemetery and memorial. One and a half km further on, you will pass Cabaret Rouge British Cemetery on your left. Descend into the valley of the Souchez River and the village of Souchez, which was destroyed in 1915. Continue through Souchez on the D937 and on the outskirts of town, turn left to the Notre-Dame de Lorette French national cemetery and memorial. It is clearly signposted.

At the top of the ridge, park in front of the cemetery and approach the panorama table.

Point 1: Notre-Dame de Lorette Ridge

The view from this position is fantastic. To the south are the ruins of Mont-St-Éloi and Arras (the "beffroi" marks the Petite-Place). Directly below you are the villages of Ablain-St-Nazaire and Carency (both destroyed in 1915). The church of Neuville-St. Vaast is visible in the distance to the southeast. Closer to you, looking in a southeasterly direction, is the village of Souchez in the valley and, behind it, the northern part of Vimy Ridge and The Pimple. You can also see Cabaret Rouge Cemetery. The best view is that of Vimy Ridge itself.

The Canadian front lines ran from 100 metres this side of The Pimple along the ridge behind Souchez. The area right of the Pimple, where the tall deciduous trees now stand, marks the location of the failed March 1st, 1917 trench raid.** On April 9th, 1917, this was the northern flank of the Canadian Corps attack. The 72nd Battalion (Seaforth

---

* There are several sites in La Targette worth visiting. One is the large French Cemetery 500 meters south of the junction. Another is the large German Cemetery (45, 000 burials) 1.3 kilometers south on the D937 towards Arras. You can also visit part of the tunnels which linked La Targette to the Vimy Ridge defensive positions. The entrance is on the east side of the D937 at the intersection of the D937 and D55.

** It is also the location of Givenchy-en-Gohelle Canadian Cemetery. See Point 3.

Highlanders of Vancouver) made a successful but costly attack against the warren of German trenches built up since 1915. The terrain was a lunar landscape.

Givenchy-en-Gohelle village is directly over Vimy Ridge behind The Pimple. The Canadian front lines followed the gradual decline of the ridge to the southwest and were only one kilometre east of the village of Neuville-St. Vaast, whose church tower can be seen in the distance five km away.

As you view the battlefield of the 1st, 2nd and 3rd Canadian Divisions from this vantage point, you might want to reflect on the nature of the fighting of 1915. Notre-Dame de Lorette was a slaughter house for both the French and Germans. Yet its significance appears to have been worth the sacrifice.

The French national memorial and cemetery are worth visiting, as is the museum at the back of the cemetery.

Return to your car and retrace your route. On the way out, notice the major centre of Lens (then a major coal mining centre) in the north and the large number of conical slag heaps (crassier) that dot the landscape. This region is very proud of its mining heritage. You will have a better view of Souchez and The Pimple as you descend the ridge.

When you reach the D937, head to Souchez. When you see the "Mairie" and signs for Givenchy-en-Gohelle Canadian Cemetery and Zouave Valley Cemetery, turn left. Pass the church, continue through the village and turn left toward Givenchy-en-Gohelle Canadian Cemetery. The road rises steeply up the ridge and many inundations from the First World War are still present on the slopes — shell holes, remnants of dugouts and tunnel entrances leading to the front line. Drive under the toll highway and turn left at the first small road. Follow the road to the end and stop your car.

Point 2: The Pimple, April 12th, 1917
You are standing on the Canadian front lines for the attack of April 12th, 1917. This area was beyond the northern flank of the Canadian Corps attack of April 9th. The German positions at The Pimple created havoc on the flank of the attacking Canadian battalions. The Notre-Dame de Lorette Ridge and the villages of Souchez, Ablain-St-Nazaire and Carency are visible to the west.

NOTRE-DAME DE LORETTE
FRENCH NATIONAL MEMORIAL AND CEMETERY

On the windswept ridge of Notre-Dame de Lorette, covering ground which was a major battlefield some eight decades ago, is the largest national cemetery of France. Located at the most spectacular position to view the heroic if costly battles of 1915, Notre-Dame de Lorette immortalizes more than 40,000 soldiers who fought and died to free their country.

Cemeteries from the First World War are evident throughout the Vimy region. There are 13 Commonwealth War Graves Commission cemeteries, predominantly Canadian soldiers killed at Vimy, a Czech cemetery (First and Second World Wars), a Polish memorial (First World War), an immense German cemetery containing almost 45,000 graves and two major French cemeteries, including the one at Notre-Dame de Lorette. The other, at La Targette, contains more than 12,000 burials.

The Notre-Dame de Lorette national cemetery was constructed between 1920 and 1925 during the battlefield clearances in Artois, Flanders and the French battlefields north of Ypres. There lie the graves of more than 20,000 French and Colonial French troops. Its ossuary contains the remains of almost 20,000 unknown soldiers. The 62-metre tower, which is topped by a powerful beacon, and the chapel were unveiled in 1925. On the ground floor of the tower are several tombs representing unknown French soldiers from the Second World War, the Indochinese (Vietnam)* War and the Algerian Civil War.

As well, there is an urn containing the ashes of some of the French who perished in labour and concentration camps during the Second World War. At the back of the cemetery is a museum.

The French used a grave-marking system quite different from that used in the Commonwealth cemeteries. A cross marks the graves of French soldiers and a tombstone inscribed with Arabic letters connotes the graves of French Colonial troops, Algerians, Moroccans, Senegalese and Indochinese.

The bleak, exposed ridge at Notre-Dame de Lorette provides the perfect place for those soldiers to rest.

* In 1987 the French Government repatriated from Vietnam the remains of more than 24,000 French casualties of the Indochinese War (1945-54). The cemetery containing the dead of the Iodochinese war is located at Frejus near Cannes.

Notre-Dame de Lorette French National Cemetery.
(PHOTO: N. CHRISTIE)

Looking east, you can see the cement skeleton of the 44th Battalion (Manitoba) Memorial in the middle of the field and, beyond it, the Bois de Givenchy. To the southeast is the rise behind which were the main German trenches of The Pimple position. The twin pylons of the Canadian national monument on Hill 145 are just over the rise.

On April 9th, 1917, The Pimple inflicted heavy casualties on the flank of the attacking Canadian battalions. The 72nd and 78th Battalions (Winnipeg Grenadiers) were particularly hard hit and many of their dead are buried in Givenchy-en-Gohelle Canadian Cemetery.

Between where you stand and the old 44th Memorial was a series of mine craters, remnants of the severe mining warfare of 1915 and 1916. The craters Football, Broadbridge, John, Mildren, Newcut and Irish created many problems for the Canadians before the attack. Today, not one inundation remains of these craters.

Of all the attacking Divisions, the 4th was nearest the German front lines (on the other side of the old 44th Memorial). This area witnessed severe fighting between French and German forces in 1915. Captured and then lost by the French, The apparently-impregnable Pimple was of major strategic importance.

The abandoned 44th Battalion Memorial on the Pimple. Givenchy Wood is in the background.
(PHOTO: N. CHRISTIE)

The Pimple and the northern part of Vimy Ridge from Notre-Dame de Lorette.
(PHOTO: N. CHRISTIE)

Following the capture of Hill 145 on April 10th, a separate attack was planned for April 12th to capture The Pimple and complete the taking of Vimy Ridge. Three battalions of the 4th Division were to be employed for this offensive. The 44th Battalion attacked toward The Pimple from where you now stand. The 50th (Alberta) and 46th (Saskatchewan) Battalions attacked north of here toward the Bois de Givenchy.

At five a.m., taking advantage of the poor visibility in driving snow, they stormed the German trenches. By daybreak, the position was in their hands. On the night of April 12th-13th, the Germans withdrew from Givenchy and retreated to prepared positions further east on the Douai Plain.

Return to your car and drive back toward the overpass. At the junction, turn left and ascend the ridge. Stop at Givenchy-en-Gohelle Canadian Cemetery.

Point 3: The Flank of the 4th Division attack, April 9th, 1917

This heavily wooded, slightly sunken area[*] is where the 72nd Battalion advanced through a warren of trenches to protect the flank of the Canadian Corps. The 38th Battalion (Eastern Ontario) attacked south of the 72nd and, similarly, was caught up in the trench maze. The 38th also suffered from machine gun fire, not only from The Pimple, but also from Hill 145. The 87th Battalion (Grenadier Guards of Montreal) on the right of the 38th had failed to achieve its objectives early April 9th, allowing the German machine gunners to focus on the advance of the 38th.

Walk along the rough track and observe the forested area to your right, where trenches and shell holes are still visible amid the foliage. You can get a very good impression of this old battlefield and the trench system that opposed these Canadian units. About 200 metres along the track, you will come to the spot where Captain Thain MacDowell[**] performed his heroic deeds to help maintain the costly gains made by the 38th Battalion.

---

[*] This also marks the failed trench raid of March 1,1917.
[**] Born in Lachute, Quebec on September 16, 1880; died in Nassau, Bahamas on March 29,1960.

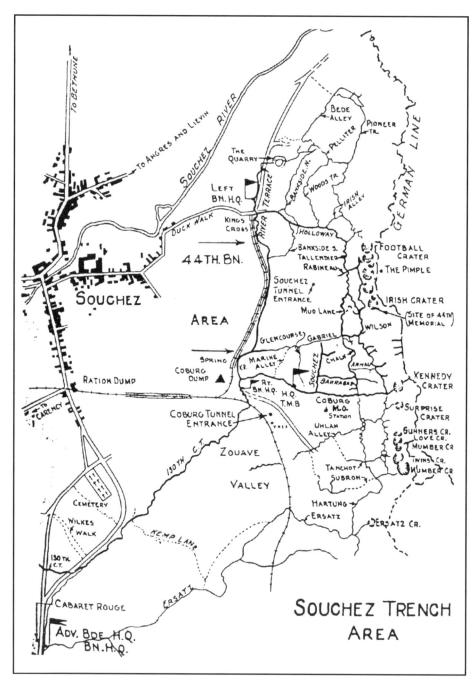

The Pimple.

Top: View of Hill 145 from Givenchy Road Cemetery. (PHOTO: N. CHRISTIE)
Bottom: Hill 145 (The Canadian Monument) from The Pimple. The trees to the right mark the position of Givenchy-en-Gohelle Canadian Cemetery. (PHOTO: N. CHRISTIE)

MacDowell and two runners snaked through the trench works and captured two German machine guns who were holding up the advance. They held the important position for five days against German counter-attacks. MacDowell was awarded the Victoria Cross for "conspicuous bravery and indomitable resolution in face of heavy machine gun and shellfire."

The 38th drove a salient into the German positions and by the following day their position had been secured.

Continue along the path beside the soccer field as far as the Givenchy road (D55). From here, there is a clear view of the Vimy Memorial on Hill 145. Now, you should be able to put this part of the battle into perspective and understand why the failure of the 87th Battalion in the centre created such problems.

Hill 145 remained in German hands until the untried Pioneer Battalion, the 85th (Nova Scotia Highlanders), launched a desperate attack across the fields to the south. The men surged across the field of fire and somehow managed to take the German trenches on the Hill. Not bad for a first action! The next day, April 10th, two battalions of the 4th Division secured the position (see *Point 6.*)

The view of Givenchy village and the Douai Plain is exceptional from here. Return to the cemetery. A second line of massive mine craters — Montreal,* Momber, Love and Gunner Craters — ran north of here, across the road from the cemetery. Kennedy Crater was 150 metres north of Gunner.

Return to your car and head back to Souchez. On the outskirts of the village, turn left and follow the signs to Zouave Valley Cemetery. Drive to the cemetery and stop.

Point 4: Zouave Valley

Zouave Valley was considered the safe spot and was a hive of activity in 1916 and 1917. Light gauge railways, ammunition dumps and support troops inhabited the dugouts and tunnels still vaguely visible in the sides of the ridge. Neuville-St. Vaast is 2.5 km south of the cemetery and there is an excellent view of Notre-Dame de Lorette. The valley is named after the French Zouaves who fought the Germans here in ferocious battle in 1915.

---

* This is the actual location of Montreal Crater. The sign in the crater at the preserved trenches in Vimy Park is incorrect.

The Vimy Memorial - Canada mourning her Dead

Return to your car and drive back to Souchez. When the road meets the D937, turn left for Neuville-St. Vaast and Arras. At La Targette, turn left on the D49 to Neuville-St. Vaast. From the village centre, follow the signs to the Vimy Canadian National monument on the D55. On the outskirts of the village, off to your right in the middle of a farmer's field, is the grave of a French officer killed in 1915.

In the Canadian Park, turn right into the parking lot for the tour of the trenches. Park your car here. A visit to the trenches and a tour of the Grange Tunnel is an excellent way to get a feel for the fighting in this area.[*]

The large craters visible in the park indicate the severity of mining warfare on the Ridge. As with the positions at The Pimple, mine warfare played a dominant role in 1915 and 1916. Mines were also used in 1917 but not to the same degree.

In theory, following a mine explosion, the men would rush the position, capture and entrench the far lip of the crater, by that gaining valuable land and extinguishing a significant German position. However, the Germans often reacted faster than anticipated and mines rarely blew exactly where they were supposed to, often inflicting casualties on their own men. Consequently, the two forces would oppose each other from opposite ends of a massive crater and everything would settle down again. Such was the case in the Vimy area, as can be seen from the trench positions. The 3rd Division's 42nd Battalion (Black Watch of Montreal), Royal Canadian Regiment and Princess Patricia's Canadian Light Infantry attacked across these fields on April 9th, 1917.

Walk back to the main road and turn right. Continue for 200 metres, cross the road to Thélus and Vimy, and stop at the large crater 50 metres further on, on the right side of the road.

Point 5: Broadmarsh Crater, 3rd and 4th Divisions

This large crater, known as Broadmarsh Crater, was the boundary of the attack by the 3rd and 4th Divisions on April 9th. To orient yourself, Hill 145 is 500 metres straight up the road. The crater line, where the 3rd Division attacked, is visible through the trees. Canadian Cemetery No. 2 is to the northwest at the end of the road. Depending on the season, you might be able to see the French national monument on Notre-Dame de Lorette.

[*] Canadian Student Guides offer guided tours between April and November.

View of Vimy Ridge from Cabaret Rouge British Cemetery: The Bois de Givenchy and The Pimple are on the left. Montreal Crater was near the tall trees, mid right. Givenchy-en-Gohelle Canadian cemetery is located in the trees. (PHOTO: N. CHRISTIE)

The plan for the attack sector was as follows: the 42nd Battalion south of the road, the Princess Patricia's Canadian Light Infantry at the crater line and the Royal Canadian Regiment south of them. The total attack frontage for all three battalions was 600 metres. Their objective was La Folie Wood.

North of the road, the 4th Division attacked with the 102nd (North British Columbians) and 87th Battalions. The 54th (Kootenay) and 75th (Mississauga Horse) Battalions were to follow up and pass through the attacks of the former battalions.

The attack began at 5:30 a.m. on Easter Monday. South of the road, the men stormed through the German front line positions and drove through La Folie Wood. Nevertheless, as the day progressed, it became apparent their success had outstripped the gains of the 4th Division north of the road.

Severe enfilade fire from Hill 145 inflicted severe casualties on the 42nd Battalion, forcing them to form a defensive flank on the edge of La Folie Wood.

Meanwhile, disaster had befallen the attack north of the road. The 102nd Battalion successfully captured their objectives and the 54th was able to continue the advance. This successful start for the British Columbians took place through and north of where you now stand. Unfortunately, the 87th Battalion was stopped cold with heavy casualties. The attack failed roughly where the Canadian No. 2 Cemetery lies.

With the supporting 75th Battalion also at a standstill, the Germans poured machine gun fire into the flanks of the British Columbians. The 54th Battalion withdrew. By the afternoon, small parties of Canadians had dislodged the Germans and put the attack back on track, but the losses were severe.

The 87th Battalion suffered 299 casualties, of which 155 were dead, and the toll for the more successful 102nd was 341 casualties, including 152 dead or missing. Many of the men who fell that Easter Monday are buried in Canadian Cemetery No. 2, marking the fateful battlefield of the 87th and 75th Battalions.

A visit to the cemetery and Givenchy Road Cemetery just south of it is well worth the time. As you approach them, you will see opposite Givenchy Road Cemetery a cutting up to the monument. These were the German defence positions. Mont-St-Éloi is to the west.

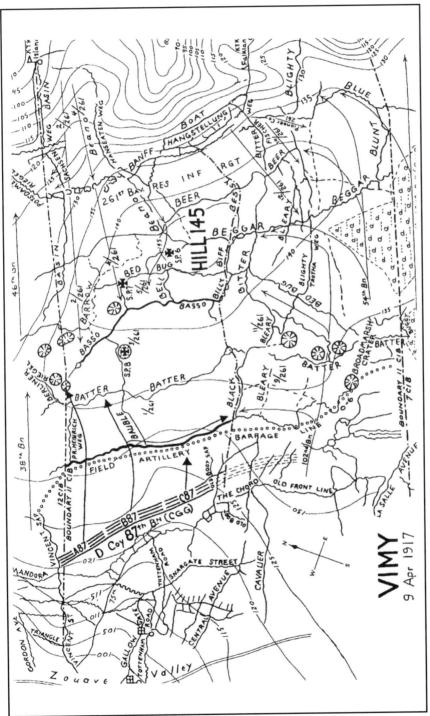

The failure in front of Hill 145.

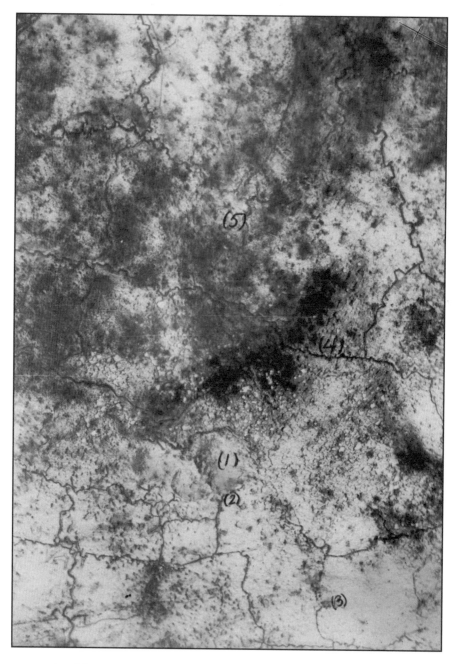

Aerial Reconnaissance February 1917, the Northern Sector of Vimy Ridge.
(1) Montreal Crater; (2) B1 Sap; (3) Ersatz Trench (4) Clutch Trench; (5) Kluck Trench

Return to your car and drive to the Canadian National Memorial. Park in the parking lot. If you look toward the Vimy Park manager's residence, you will see the village of Neuville-St. Vaast through the cutting and many old German trenches running across the field. These and the enormous number of shell holes clearly indicate the extent of the defences the Germans had at their disposal. Walk up to the Vimy Memorial.

Point 6: Hill 145, The Vimy Memorial, 4th Division

You have approached the memorial from the back. This point on Hill 145 ties together the actions of the previous points. Here is where they all converge.

The Pimple is visible to the north. The men of the 38th Battalion and Captain MacDowell fought out of the woods across from the monument. To the southwest you can see Mont-St-Éloi and, much closer, the scene where the attacking 75th and 87th Battalions were stopped and later recommenced their advance to the summit. Neuville-St. Vaast, where the 3rd Division advanced, is south southwest. South of the monument is La Folie Wood, where the men from British Columbia fought for possession along with the 3rd Division. Looking east, you can see why this position was so valuable. The Douai Plain, Lens and the coal mines were battlefields of another day.

With the ranks of the 87th Battalion and her sister battalion depleted and the Germans still in control of Hill 145, the situation was precarious. German counterattacks were threatening the Canadian successes.

The 85th Battalion, which arrived in France in February 1917 to serve as a Pioneer Battalion, digging trenches and constructing facilities, was chosen to deliver the attack. Now they had the opportunity, in their first action, to determine the success of the Vimy battle.

At six p.m., without an artillery barrage and with little knowledge of the positions they were attacking, the men from Nova Scotia advanced from the captured German front line trenches 500 metres west of where you stand.

They moved overland, surprising the Germans and, in a brief but bloody fight, captured the enemy positions at Hill 145. These German trenches are still visible today, crossing the fields west of the monument. The flanks were now saved from the enfilade fire from Hill 145. German trenches on the eastern edge of the ridge, however, continued to hold out. But the fighting of April 9th was over.

The Vimy Memorial - The Sympathy of the Canadians for the Helpless

Walk around to the front of the memorial which overlooks the Douai Plain.

On April 10th, the 44th and 50th Battalions drove the Germans permanently off the ridge. The 44th attacked south of the monument and the 50th north of it. At 3:15 p.m., they moved across the grassed area surrounding the monument and approached the German positions at the edge of the ridge. After a short fight, Vimy Ridge was in Canadian hands.

The April 10th action again owed its success to individual acts of bravery such as that of Private John Pattison of the 50th Battalion. When the 50th's attack was held up, the 42-year-old private singlehandedly attacked the German machine gun position. He crossed over open ground and threw grenades at the emplacement. Then he attacked and killed the five surviving crew members with his bayonet. His bravery allowed the advance to resume.

The 50th successfully pushed the Germans off the ridge and pursued them to its foot. Looking northeast and east, you can see where this courageous attack took place. Pattison, who was awarded a Victoria Cross for his bravery, performed his feat roughly 300 metres north of where you stand. Unfortunately he was killed on June 3rd, 1917 during the fighting near La Coulotte on the Douai Plain. He is buried in La Chaudière Military Cemetery.

You may want to follow the two-km trail through La Folie Wood, where there remains much evidence of the fighting. The entrance is on the south side of the ring road and the track takes you over the ridge toward Vimy village.

Return to your car and drive back toward the Trenches. Turn left after Broadmarsh Crater and follow the road to Vimy and Thélus, signposted "Gendarmerie." You will pass by "the Trenches" on your right. This was the area captured by the 3rd Division on April 9th. After 1.2 km, you will pass a small sign indicating the 3rd Canadian Division Memorial. It is 100 metres into the wood to your left. It was built on the location of La Folie Farm.

This area was captured by the 2nd and 4th Battalions Canadian Mounted Rifles on April 9th. The terrain in the wood is extremely cut up and trenches are still clearly visible through the trees.

Continue on the road until you meet the N17. Turn right for Thélus. In the fields off to your right, you can see Thélus Military

Cemetery, which contains the bodies of many of those killed at Vimy. Continue along the N17 for 800 metres as far as the traffic lights. *Immediately before the lights*, turn right onto the small farm road cutting between the trees and houses. Follow the narrow paved road for one km to Lichfield Crater Cemetery. Stop your car and go into the cemetery.

Point 7: Lichfield Crater - The attack of the 2nd Division

Walk around the cemetery until you are behind the Cross of Sacrifice in the seating area. Stand on the stone benches.

This unusually-designed cemetery was built around Lichfield Crater. The 24th Battalion (Queen Victoria's Rifles of Montreal) attacked here on April 9th, 1917. They drove across the ground to the east and broke into the German second line, the Zwischen Stellung, 600 metres distant. The small road 400 metres to the north marks the boundary between the attacks of the 2nd and 3rd Divisions. The 24th and 26th (New Brunswick) Battalions attacked from Lichfield Crater to this road.

The battalions of the 3rd Division — the 1st Canadian Mounted Rifles (Saskatchewan), 2nd Canadian Mounted Rifles (British Columbia) and the 4th Canadian Mounted Rifles (Central Ontario) — attacked north of the road. They advanced toward the northern extension of Zwischen Stellung and La Folie Wood.

Further north, about one kilometre distant (out of view), the attack of the 4th Canadian Mounted Rifles was linked to the attack by the Royal Canadian Regiment at the crater line. South of the 24th Battalion attack, the 19th Battalion (Central Ontario) was pushing north of the highway overpass.

The 2nd Division's attack linked with the 1st Division south of the overpass (see *Point 8)*. This is the best vantage point from which to view the centre of the Canadian attack on Vimy Ridge.

Look southwest toward Arras. Mont-St-Éloi, the village of Neuville-St. Vaast and, one km south of the village in open fields, the French memorial to the 1915 fighting at The Labyrinthe are clearly visible. Just west of the overpass is Zivy Crater Cemetery. North is Notre-Dame de Lorette and La Folie Wood. East is Thélus Military Cemetery and Thélus church. Zwischen Stellung ran north/south 100 metres west of Thélus Military Cemetery.

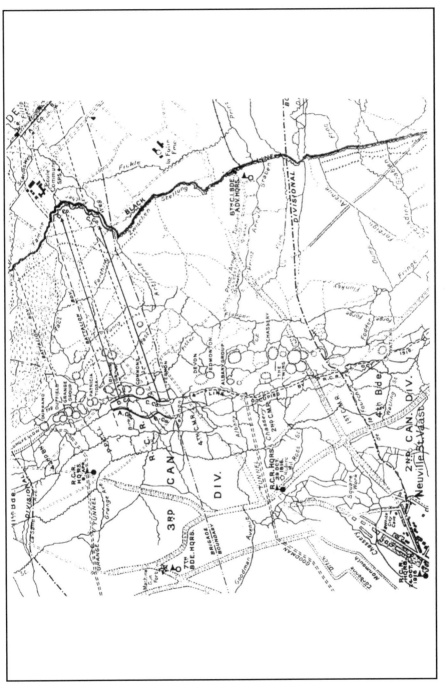

The area of the 3rd Division attack, 9 April, 1917

The 3rd Division's Memorial at La Folie Farm. It reads:

"3rd Canadian Division
To glory of God and in everlasting memorial of our gallant
comrades who gave their lives in the defence of the line
from October 23rd 1916 to February 15th 1917 and in the
attack and capture of Vimy Ridge on April 9th 1917 and in
the subsequent operations."

(PHOTO: N. CHRISTIE)

On April 9th, 1917, the 24th and 19th Battalions advanced quickly and captured the German front line positions. The attack went well until they closed with the Germans holding the second line, Zwischen Stellung. At this point, 400 metres east of you, the opposition stiffened and the fighting became severe. The artillery had done its job before the battle but now small groups of attackers faced German machine guns and entrenched positions. Within 30 minutes, the 24th Battalion was in Zwischen Stellung.

The 22nd Battalion (Canadien-français), who were mopping up, faced pockets of Germans who had been bypassed or who were still holding on to the main trench. Successful as the battle was for the 24th Battalion, the cost was indeed heavy. Seventy-one men were dead and another 165 were wounded or missing.

A direct hit on a German gun emplacement in Vimy Village, April 1917.
(PUBLIC ARCHIVES OF CANADA)

The 25th Battalion (Nova Scotia) followed through the 24th and drove east, past Thélus Military Cemetery, across the Vimy-Arras road (N17) and into the third line trench (Turko Graben). To the north, the Canadian Mounted Rifle Brigade of the 3rd Division was also successful in pushing into La Folie Wood, capturing La Folie Farm and digging in on the eastern edge of the ridge.

This isolated point is the best location for sensing a flow of the Battle of Vimy and absorbing the historical atmosphere.

Return to your car and go back to the main road (N17). Turn right toward Arras. You are traversing the battlefield of the 1st Canadian Division. William Milne, whose heroic deeds early in the morning of April 9th earned a Victoria Cross, was killed this side of the overpass, off to your left.

After 1.1 km, you pass Nine Elms Military Cemetery which contains the graves of many Canadians killed on that day. Milne performed his heroic action in the field west of the cemetery. After a further 500 metres, you pass Arras Road Cemetery, continue on to Ecurie, turn right and right again onto a small road leading to the cemetery. Stop and walk into the cemetery.

Point 8: The attack of the 1st Division - Arras Road Military Cemetery
There are two main views of the battlefield from this cemetery. For the first, walk to the northwest corner. The cemetery is midway between the German front line trenches (Eisener Kreuz Weg) and their second position (Zwolfer Stellung) east of the N17. Northwest of the cemetery is Neuville-St. Vaast. The fields over which the Canadians attacked on April 9th are to the north, toward the overpass connecting the villages of Neuville-St. Vaast and Thélus. With binoculars you can view both Lichfield and Zivy Crater Cemeteries.

The 18th Battalion (Western Ontario) attacked south of the overpass. They were supported by, from north to south, the 16th (Canadian Scottish), 14th (Royal Montreal Regiment), 15th (48th Highlanders of Toronto), 10th (Alberta) and, through the cemetery, 7th (British Columbia) Battalions.

The 5th Battalion (Saskatchewan), the right flanking battalion of the Canadian Corps, attacked northwards from the junction where the trenches cut across the N17, 500 metres south of the cemetery.

The Vimy Memorial - The Defenders and the breaking of the sword

Protecting the flank of the Canadians was the British 51st (Highland) Division. Similar to the attack north of the overpass, this advance also went well initially, with small unit actions required to eliminate German machine gun positions and trench defences. All across the fields north of you, regardless of cost, the Canadians surged forward.

Vimy is generally perceived as a walkover and it was a steady advance, but the losses were very high. With few exceptions, battalions would suffer 100 dead of the 600 to 700 men attacking. This translates to a one-in-six chance of being killed. Chances of being wounded were about one in three. This is an astounding observation of the mental and physical state of the soldiers who, despite deadly opposition, were willing to advance.

The surge forward found the men in Zwischen Stellung, one km from the jump-off lines, by seven a.m. Again, individual acts of bravery redeemed difficult situations. When the attack of the 18th Battalion (at the overpass) was held up by German machine guns, Lance Sergeant Ellis Sifton charged a machine gun singlehandedly, killing all the crew. He then drove off a group of Germans advancing along the trench and was killed. Sifton* was awarded the Victoria Cross for his bravery.

South of the 18th Battalion, the 16th ran into similar problems. This is where Private William Milne faced a machine gun position and killed the crew with grenades. He then repeated his action on a second German machine gun post and was killed shortly afterwards. For his bravery, Private Milne** was awarded the Victoria Cross. The attack swept across the N17 and into the German defences at Thélus.

Walk to the southeast corner of the cemetery. The view from here covers the attack of the 5th and 7th Battalions. Both units were successful but, like the others, suffered heavily. The 7th Battalion had 87 men killed, most of whom are buried in this cemetery.

You can also get a clear view of Ecurie, Roclincourt (scene of fighting by the 51st Division), the Scarpe River Valley and, on the other side of the river, the village on the mound, Monchy-le-Preux.

---

* Born at Wallacetown, Ontario, October 12,1881, died Neuville-St. Vaast, France on April 9, 1917. Surprisingly, Sifton is buried in Lichfield Crater and is the only member of the 18th to be buried there. Most of the 18th Battalion, which had 41 men killed that day, are buried in Zivy Crater.
** Born at Wishaw, Scotland, December21, 1892; died Neuville-St. Vaast, France, April 9, 1917. Milne's body was never identified. He is commemorated by name on the Vimy Memorial.

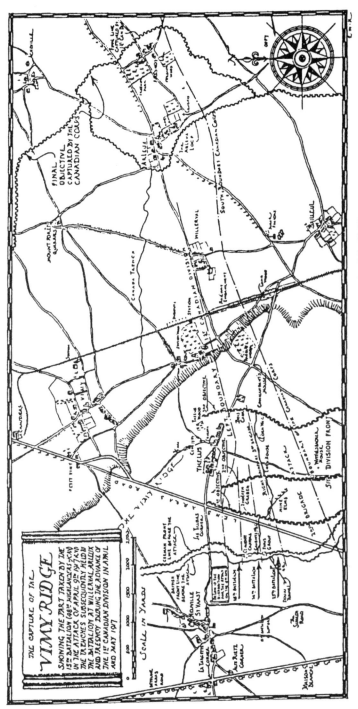

The Front of the First Canadian Division, April 9, 1917.

Walk to the northeast end of the cemetery. From here you can see Thélus village and the fields across which the Canadians extended their attack. After overcoming the front lines, Zwischen Stellung (one km east) was captured. At this point the 1st (Western Ontario), 4th (Central Ontario) and 3rd (Toronto Regiment) Battalions took over the attack and drove south of Thélus toward Farbus.

Using binoculars, look northeast, a km east of Thélus. East of the wood (Bois Carré) is a large cross. The cross is the memorial (*Point 9*) to the 1st Division and commemorates their fallen. The original was erected in December 1917.

Return to your car and drive back to Les Tilleuls. Turn right at the traffic lights (the Canadian Artillery Memorial, unveiled by Arthur Currie, is across the road) on the D49 to Thélus. You are driving over the territory captured by the 21st (Eastern Ontario) Battalion, who took over the attack from the 18th and 19th Battalions. Drive through Thélus, the scene of fighting by the 31st (Alberta) and the 28th (Saskatchewan) on April 9th. On the outskirts of the village, you will pass Bois Carré British Cemetery which contains many Canadians killed on that day. Just after the small Bois Carré, you come to a large wooden cross in the fields on your right. Park your car and walk to the memorial along the grassed access path.

Point 9: The follow-up attacks of the 1st and 2nd Divisions, April 9th, 1917, Thélus/Bois Carré
This area was captured by the 3rd Battalion on April 9th and from here we overlook the battlefield discussed at *Point 8*. You can see Arras Road Cemetery, and the villages of Ecurie, Roclincourt, the city of Arras, the valley of the Scarpe River and so on. Binoculars will be a real advantage here.

The 1st, 3rd and 4th Battalions attacked across the ground southeast of you and, upon reaching the ridge, the 3rd continued the assault to capture Farbus Wood 900 metres to the east. The fields north of Thélus were the objective of the second stage of the attack by the 29th (British Columbia), 28th and 31st Battalions. Hill 135, 600 metres north of Thélus, was captured by the Royal West Kents and Kings Own Scottish Borderers of the 5th Imperial Division, attached to the Canadian Corps

Canadians consolidating their positions on Vimy Ridge, April 1917.

(PUBLIC ARCHIVES OF CANADA)

General Sir Arthur Currie unveiling the Canadian Artillery Memorial at Les Tilleuls, February 1918.

(PUBLIC ARCHIVES OF CANADA)

The 1st Canadian Division's Memorial East of Thélus. It reads:

*"In proud memory of all
soldiers of the First
Canadian Division who
fell in the investment,
assault and defence of
the Vimy Ridge March 4th,
April 9th and July 23rd A.D.
1917. This mark is set by
their comrades in arms
Gloria-in-Excelsis Deo
Christmas 1917"*

for the battle. North of the road, the 27th (City of Winnipeg) and the 29th Battalions continued a third phase of the attack, driving into Goulot Wood (one km north of you) west of Farbus.

Later in the day, the Canadian Light Horse tried to exploit the break-through by reconnoitring through Farbus to Willerval where severe machine-gun fire sent them scurrying for cover. By nightfall on April 9th, the advance of the 1st and 2nd Canadian Divisions had captured more than three km of heavily defended German trenches, an area thought impregnable by the Germans. It was an important victory.

You have now completed the tour of the Vimy battlefield.

To return to Arras, follow the D49 through Thélus and turn left at the traffic lights on the N17. If you wish to tour the Arleux and Fresnoy battlefields, stay on the D49.

Herds of Germans surrendering to the Canadians, April 1917.
(PUBLIC ARCHIVES OF CANADA)

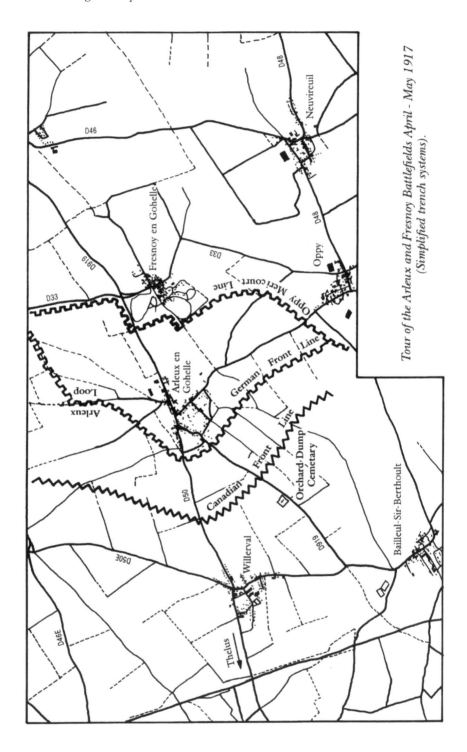

Tour of the Arleux and Fresnoy Battlefields April - May 1917 (Simplified trench systems).

THE DRIVING TOUR
of The Battle Of The Arleux Loop, April 28th, 1917
and Fresnoy, May 3rd, 1917

Leave the Grand'Place, following road signs for Lens and Vimy. Follow the N17 past Roclincourt, Arras Road and Nine Elms Cemeteries, pass under the toll highway overpass and, at the lights (the junction with the D49), turn right for Thélus. Turn left for Farbus on the D50. Continue through Farbus and Willerval (where the Canadian Light Horse was turned back on April 9th) and stop 1.3 km from Willerval, outside the village of Arleux-en-Gohelle.

The opening day, April 9th, 1917, of the Battle of Arras 1917 was a tremendous success. From Hill 145 to Croiselles south of Arras, British and Canadian troops broke through German defences. By April 14th, they had advanced more than six kilometres. However, the heady days of success quickly ended as the German line stiffened. During the next month, major attacks in the Second Battle of the Scarpe April 23rd/24th and the Third Battle of the Scarpe May 3rd yielded little success for very heavy casualties. The only successes of those battles were at Arleux and Fresnoy, both Canadian operations.

The Battle of Arras was a failed opportunity, only too typical of the First World War. The British Army suffered 140,000 killed, wounded and missing, of which more than 20,000 were Canadian. After the capture of The Pimple and Hill 145, the Germans withdrew onto the Douai Plain, conceding the ridge. They established themselves in a well-constructed defensive system called the Oppy-Méricourt Line. Part of the main system included a defensive loop surrounding the fortified village of Arleux-en-Gohelle.

After the German withdrawal, the Canadians pushed their front line 600 metres east of the village of Willerval. As part of the Second Battle of the Scarpe, the Canadians were to capture the Arleux Loop. Three battalions of the 1st Division, the 8th (90th Rifles of Winnipeg), 10th (Alberta) and 5th, attacked south to north respectively of the village. The 25th Battalion attacked 1200 metres north of the village.

At 4:25 a.m. on April 28th, they advanced through uncut German barbed wire into the village. By six a.m., Arleux was completely in Canadian hands. Surprised at the success of the Canadian attack, the

View of Vimy Ridge from the eastern plain. Hill 145 (The Canadian Memorial) is visible mid-left and Givenchy village, The Pimple and Bois de Givenchy on the right. (PHOTO: N. CHRISTIE)

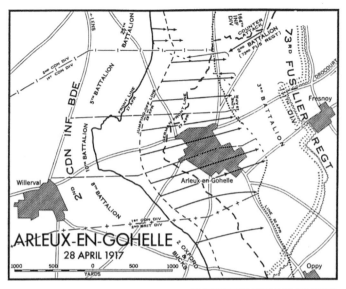

(DEPATMENT OF NATIONAL DEFENCE)

Germans prepared counterattacks but each time, heavy artillery fire from Vimy Ridge broke the German assault.

One thousand Canadians were killed, wounded or missing during this action.

You are standing on what was No Man's Land amidst the German barbed wire. The 10th Battalion attacked astride the road on which you are now standing. The 8th Battalion captured the south part of the village and attacked south of you over the rise. North of the road, the 5th and 25th Battalions advanced across the fields. The 25th Battalion's attack was held up in the sunken road north of Arleux.

Return to your car and continue along the D50 toward Arleux. Along the first road, on the left, is the sunken road where the 25th Battalion stopped on April 28th, 1917. At the village center, turn right on the D919. You are driving through the area of the 8th Battalion attack. After 1.3 km outside the village, stop at Orchard Dump Cemetery.

From the hill behind the cemetery, you can get a clear view of the Arleux battlefield. To the southwest are Oppy and Oppy Wood. Due east is Fresnoy village, wood and park.

Return to your car and drive back to Arleux. Turn right on the D919 to Bois-Bernard and stop 700 metres out of the village.

LANCELOT EDGAR ASHCROFT

LIEUTENANT, *16th Battalion, C.E.F.*

Was born in Hunterville, New Zealand, in January, 1897. Two years later he came to British Columbia with his parents. He received his education in the Isle of Man, Victoria, B.C., New Zealand, and at Vernon, B.C. He then entered the service of the Bank of Montreal at the latter place. Early in 1916 he enlisted in the 103rd Battalion, Canadian Infantry, in which he was given his commission as Lieutenant, and went overseas with his unit. While training in England he was appointed Orderly Officer on the Headquarters Staff at Seaford, where he remained until March, 1917. He then went to France and was posted to the 16th Battalion, Canadian Scottish. A few days after he reached the front he was killed by enemy fire on the morning of April 9th, 1917, while going forward with his battalion in the attack for the capture of Vimy Ridge.

ROBERT ALDHAM WILSON

PRIVATE, *50th Battalion, C.E.F.*

Was born in Fort Vermilion, Alberta, on January 4th, 1893. He received his education at the High School in Bowmanville, Ontario, and in September, 1910, he entered the service of the Hudson's Bay Company at Fort Vermilion, where he remained for a year and a half. He then joined the staff of the Bank of Montreal and at the time of his enlistment he was employed in the Edmonton, Alberta, branch. Previous to his enlisting for overseas service, he was attached to the 101st Regiment. In March, 1916, he enlisted as a Private in the 138th Battalion. He proceeded overseas with this unit and after a considerable period of training in England, he went to France. He had been in the line only a few months when he was instantly killed in action on April 10th, 1917, in an attack during the Canadian offensive in front of Vimy Ridge.

THE BATTLE OF FRESNOY, MAY 3rd, 1917

After the battle on April 28th, the Canadians held a position 400 meters east of Arleux. They had captured the outer loop of the Oppy-Méricourt line. The next objective was to bite off a piece of the main line at Fresnoy hamlet in an attack which was part of another major British offensive, the Third Battle of the Scarpe. Just like the second battle, the British attack hit a stone wall. The only tangible success was at Fresnoy.*

The Canadian plan was for the 3rd Battalion to attack the wood of the hamlet, the 2nd (Eastern Ontario) to drive into the hamlet and the 1st to advance into the park to the north (astride the road on which you are now standing). In the fields north of the hamlet, the 27th and the 31st Battalions would protect the flank of the 1st Division's attack.

However, unlike Arleux, Fresnoy was crucial to the German plans and any success by the Canadians was sure to meet immediate German counterattacks. Moreover, the Germans were ready.

The Canadians moved into position during the early morning of May 3rd and were shelled by the Germans, resulting in some casualties. At 3:45 a.m., the Canadian Artillery opened fire and a few minutes later, the men of the 1st Division advanced, capturing the wood and breaking into the hamlet. By six a.m., they had captured Fresnoy and pushed their line 250 metres east.

The attack of the 27th successfully broke into the German lines, but initially ran into difficulties. Again, the bravery of individuals saved the day. The northern part of the attack broke through the German lines but was isolated by the complete failure of the 31st Battalion on the left. Although surrounded, one small unit succeeded in turning their attack on the Germans and captured the German line from behind! The southern flank of the 27th Battalion was held back initially, but another small group of five men, commanded by Lieutenant Robert Coombe, broke into the German trench. Coombe consolidated the gain and went on to capture 280 metres of the German trench. He was later killed by a sniper. Coombe's** brave actions, which earned him the Victoria Cross, saved the flank of the Canadian attack.

---

* The Australians attacked with some success, breaking into Hindenburg Line near Bullecourt. Fighting Continued there for two weeks.

** Born at Aberdeen, Scotland, August 5, 1880; died Fresnoy, May 3, 1917. Coombe's body was never recovered and he is commemorated by name on the Vimy Memorial. In all probability, his remains and those of other Canadians were buried by the Germans, a standard method of disposing of enemy dead employed by both sides.

Drive to Fresnoy and turn right on the D33 into the hamlet. Coombe's courageous attack took place 350 metres north, directly east of the D33 to Acheville. The wooded park to your right was captured by the 1st Battalion. In the village, turn right on the Rue d'Arleux and drive around the church area. This was where the 2nd Battalion entered the hamlet.

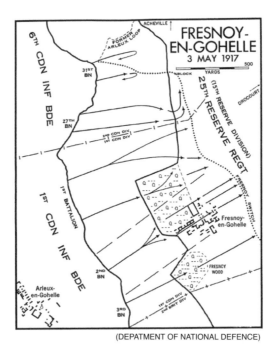

(DEPATMENT OF NATIONAL DEFENCE)

The Germans attempted two major counterattacks on Fresnoy. Both were smashed by artillery and small arms fire, but heavy German artillery fire continued throughout the day, inflicting many casualties. On May 5th, the Canadians were relieved by British troops in Fresnoy. This tremendous success shocked the Germans, but the Canadians had paid with 1,259 killed, wounded or missing.

Determined to regain this lost brick of their main defences, the Germans launched a devastating attack on British troops in Fresnoy on May 8th. By the evening, Fresnoy was lost and the front line was pushed back toward Arleux.

Drive through the hamlet to the cemetery. Directly west of here was where the 3rd Battalion attacked and captured Fresnoy Wood. Turn around and return to the D50, drive through Willerval and Farbus and turn left to Thélus on the D49. At the traffic lights, turn left on the N17 and return to Arras.

German Prisoners and Canadian Red Cross men assist in dispatching of wounded on a light railway, Vimy Ridge, April 1917.

(PUBLIC ARCHIVES OF CANADA)

THE STORM OF STEEL

Ernst Jünger's account of his experiences as an officer of the 73rd Hanoverian Fusiliers, 1915-1918, has become a classic First World War story as viewed from the German side.

"The Storm of Steel," with its "German" attitude of viewing the battlefield almost as an arena for a martial sport, certainly contains the horror of the war and, on a few occasions, reveals his nerves of steel.

He writes in detail of the ferocity of the shelling at the Battle of the Arleux loop on April 28, 1917, and at Passchendaele. Both times he was opposite Canadian attacks.

His view from the opposite side of the attack on Arleux is an interesting one:

"So I lay down again, hoping to be all the better prepared for the expected exertions. However, as I was just falling asleep a shell hit the house and blew in the wall of the cellar stairs and threw the masonry into the cellar. We jumped up and hurried into the dugout.

"...I lit a cigar and went into the smoke-filled cellar. In the middle of it there was a heap of wreckage — bedsteads, straw mattresses, and various pieces of furniture, all in fragments and piled nearly up to the roof. After we had put a few candles on ledges of the walls, we set to work. Catching hold of the limbs that stuck out from the wreckage, we pulled out the dead bodies. One had the head struck off, and the neck on the trunk was like a great sponge of blood. From the arm stumps of another the broken bones projected, and the uniform was saturated by a large wound in the chest. The entrails of the third poured out from a wound in the belly. As we pulled out the last a splintered board caught in the ghastly wound with a hideous noise.

"The orderly made a comment on this, and was reproved by my batman with these words: 'Best hold your tongue. In such matters talking nonsense serves no purpose.'

"...At 5:15 a.m. the fire increased to an incredible violence. Our dugout rocked and trembled like a ship on a stormy sea. All round resounded the rending of masonry and the crash of collapsing houses.

"...We had scarcely realized the great losses suffered by the regiment, when the shelling was renewed with increasing fury. My batman was standing, the last of all, on the top step of the dugout stairs, when a crash like thunder announced that the English [editor's note: they were actually Canadians] had at last succeeded in knocking in our cellar. The trusty Knigge got a good squared building-stone on the back but was not hurt. Above, everything was shot to blazes. Daylight came to us past two bicycles squeezed into the dugout entrance. We made ourselves as small as we could on the lowest step, while heavy explosions and the din of falling masonry convinced us of the insecurity of our refuge.

"...In Fresnoy the shells were sending up the earth in fountains as high as church towers. Each seemed bent on outdoing its predecessor. As though by magic, one house after another was sucked into the earth. Walls collapsed, gables fell, and bare rafters were flung through the air to mow the roofs of neighbouring houses. Clouds of splinters danced above whitish swathes of vapour. Eye and ear hung as though entranced upon this dance of destruction.

"...Stark and still, and wrapped in a ground-sheet, Lieutenant Lemière, the commander of the 8th Company, lay at the entrance, his large horn spectacles still on his nose. His men had brought him there. He was shot in the mouth. His younger brother was killed a few months later in exactly the same way."

CEMETERIES AND MEMORIALS

The remains of more than 600,000 Commonwealth servicemen lie buried in some 3,500 cemeteries carved quaintly into the rolling hills and farmers' fields of northern France and Belgium.

Landscaped and constructed during the 1920s by the Imperial War Graves Commission (now the Commonwealth War Graves Commission), these cemeteries have frozen the history of the First World War.

The principles of the IWGC, established in 1917 to maintain the cemeteries and record the Commonwealth* dead of the Great War (and later the Second World War), were threefold:

I. The name of each serviceman who died in the war or during the immediate postwar period would be commemorated on a headstone or engraved on a battlefield memorial.

II. All would receive universal treatment in death. In practice this meant a common headstone for every man regardless of rank or social standing or, in the case of those who had no grave, equal recognition on a memorial.

III. No bodies would be repatriated. All would remain in the country where they died.

The repatriation restriction and the acquisition of the land where the cemeteries originally stood have preserved for perpetuity the legacy left by the hundreds of thousands who sacrificed their lives in the Great War.

CEMETERY CATEGORIES

The types of cemeteries fall into three main categories:

I. HOSPITAL CENTRE CEMETERIES are near main hospital centres or casualty clearing stations. Burials are in chronological order and few graves are unidentified. The officers usually have a separate

---

* The term Commonwealth applies to countries of the old British Empire, namely Australia, New Zealand, India, Pakistan, Canada, South Africa, Britain and other British colonies or protectorates.

burial plot, as do Hindus, Moslems and Buddhists. Servicemen of the Jewish faith are usually buried in the Christian plots but there are exceptions. In Etaples Military Cemetery there is even a plot for black soldiers (generally of the British West Indies Regiment). It includes one Canadian.

II. REGIMENTAL OR FRONT-LINE CEMETERIES are cemeteries near the front lines for quick burial of soldiers killed at the front (trench wastage) or small battlefield cemeteries set up by Divisional or Corps Burial Officers immediately after a battle. Often the layout and rows are irregular.

III. BATTLEFIELD CLEARANCE CEMETERIES were usually small cemeteries greatly expanded after the war by the concentration of remains brought in from surrounding battlefields. They always contain a very high proportion of unidentified graves and the layout of the rows is regular and often symmetric

The cemeteries in the Vimy region reflect the Canadian occupation of this sector from October 1916 to midsummer 1918. The dead of the Battle of Vimy Ridge lie buried amongst their Commonwealth comrades, generally buried in complete plots within the cemeteries. Seventy percent of the men who died at Vimy have a known grave. The balance — the unidentified or those whose remains have yet to be found - are commemorated by name only around the base of the Vimy Memorial.

THE VIMY MEMORIAL

The Vimy Memorial, eight km north of Arras off the road to Béthune, is Canada's National Memorial erected by the people of Canada to commemorate the Canadian sacrifice in the Great War.

It also commemorates 11,285 Canadian soldiers who died in France and have no known graves. Roughly 2,000 names on the Vimy Memorial are those killed between April 9th, 1917 and May 9th, 1917. (The 6,983 who died in Belgium and have no known graves are commemorated on the Menin Gate Memorial at Ypres. The two memorials, thus, commemorate 18,268 Canadians, or 30% of all the Canadians who fell in France and Flanders during the Great War.)

REGINALD HECTOR LONGHURST
PRIVATE, *73rd Battalion, C.E.F.*

Was born in Granby, Quebec, on July 5th, 1896. After receiving his education at the High School in his native place he entered the service of the Bank of Montreal in the Cookshire branch in April, 1914. He was later employed in Sherbrooke, Three Rivers, and Montreal. In October, 1915, he enlisted as a Private in the 73rd Battalion, 5th Royal Highlanders of Canada, and went to France with his unit in the following summer. He took part in the operations on the Somme during the summer and autumn of 1916, and in the Vimy Sector in the winter of 1916-1917. After a raid near Vimy Ridge on the night of March 1st, 1917, a Lieutenant of his company was reported missing. He volunteered with two others to search for the missing officer. His two comrades came back, but he did not return. Later his body was recovered near the enemy wire.

LISLE CRADOCK RAMSAY
LIEUTENANT, *15th Battalion, C.E.F.*

Was born in Montreal, in January, 1893. He was educated at the High School, Montclair, New Jersey, and at Bishop's College School, Lennoxville, Quebec, from which he graduated. In 1910 he joined the staff of the Bank of Montreal. He enlisted in Edmonton early in July, 1915, and was given his commission as Lieutenant in the 91st Battalion, Canadian Highlanders. In the following summer he arrived in France where he was transferred to the 15th Battalion, 48th Highlanders of Canada. From the Ypres salient he went with his regiment to the Somme, where he passed through the severe fighting of the summer of 1916, then back to the Vimy sector. He was instantly killed by enemy fire on the morning of April 9th, 1917, after he had led his platoon over the top with the first wave of his battalion in the attack for the capture of Vimy Ridge.

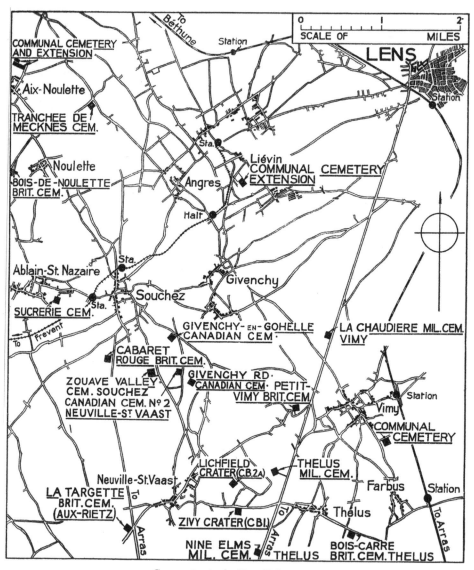

Cemeteries in the Vimy Ridge area.

The cemeteries listed below contain the majority of those who fell in the Battle of Vimy Ridge. (It is highly recommended that the Commonwealth War Graves Overprints of Michelin Maps, Nos. 51, 52 and 53 be used to help find these cemeteries. They can be obtained from the CWGC Office in Beaurains, France.)

ARRAS ROAD CEMETERY, Roclincourt

Arras Road Cemetery is five km north of Arras on the main Arras-Lens road (N17). There is no direct access from the N17, and it can only be reached via a small side road running north of Ecurie. This cemetery was created by the 2nd Canadian Infantry Brigade in April 1917. At that time, they buried 71 officers and men of the 7th Battalion (British Columbia) killed in their assault on the front line trenches on April 9th. They are in Plot I.

It was enlarged by the battlefield clearances between 1926 - 1929 and now contains the graves of 1,063 Commonwealth soldiers, 76% of whom are unidentified. Included are 111 Canadians, 25 of them unidentified. The Canadian graves were predominantly brought in from Vimy Ridge, but remains from as far away as Festubert and Fresnoy and even Cambrai are found here.

Among those buried here, in Plot III, Row O, Grave 26, is Private L. Singh of the 75th Battalion (Mississauga Horse). He was killed on October 24th, 1918. His headstone is unique to Sikhs who served with Canada in the First World War.

Also buried here is Captain Arthur Kilby, VC, MC, of the South Staffordshire Regiment, who won a posthumous Victoria Cross for bravery at Loos on September 25, 1915. Kilby, 30 when he died, is buried in Plot III, Row N, Grave 27.

The grave of Sergeant George Turner, DCM, of the 28th (Saskatchewan) Battalion was exhumed from Comines Communal Cemetery. Turner was wounded and captured in a trench raid near Kemmel, Belgium, and died in German hands. In 1929, he was re-interred in Arras Road, more than 70 km from his original place of burial.

NINE ELMS MILITARY CEMETERY, Thelus

Nine Elms Cemetery is six km north of Arras on the main Arras-Lens road, just past the Arras Road Cemetery. Access is tricky and the side road through Ecurie is the best way to reach the site. The cemetery was made by the Canadian Corps after the Battle of Vimy Ridge and originally used for the burial of 80 men of the 14th Battalion (Royal Montreal Regiment) killed on April 9th, 1917. Battlefield clearances after the war brought in many small Canadian cemeteries made by fighting units immediately after the battle.

It now contains 683 Commonwealth burials including 539 Canadians, of which 99 are unknown.

Included are soldiers of the 15th (48th Highlanders of Toronto), 16th (Western Canadian Scottish), 5th (Saskatchewan), 1st Canadian Mounted Rifles (Saskatchewan), 21st (Eastern Ontario) and the 28th (Saskatchewan) Battalions.

Sergeant John Middleton, 1st CMR is buried in Plot III, Row G, Grave 6. He was one five Scottish brothers and a cousin that resided in Medicine Hat, Alberta, who fought for Canada in the war. Three of the brothers and their brother-in-law were killed.

THELUS MILITARY CEMETERY

Thélus Cemetery is found northwest of Thélus village and 10 km north of Arras on the main Arras-Lens road. This beautiful and rarely-visited site is located 100 metres off the road in a farmer's field. It was made by the Canadian Corps in April 1917 and used until 1918.

The cemetery was originally designated C.B.8 under a numbering system used by the Canadian Corps burial officer. The "C" stands for Canadian Corps, the following letter for the Division - "A" for 1st, "B" for 2nd, "C" for 3rd, "D" for 4th - and the final number designated a specific cemetery or grave. The original burials of C.B.8 are 2nd Division and are buried in Plot II.

After the war 75 graves were brought in from the surrounding battlefield. A 3rd Division cemetery was cleared and the remains brought into Thélus. The graves re-interred here are from the 2nd (British Columbia), 4th (Toronto) and 5th (Quebec) Canadian Mounted Rifles, Royal Canadian Regiment and Princess Patricia's Canadian Light Infantry, all of the 3rd Division.

It now contains 295 Commonwealth burials, of which 245 are Canadian, 33 unidentified.

Sergeant Albert Denis, aged 27, and Private Henri Denis, aged 22, both of the 22nd Battalion (Canadien-français), are buried in Plot I, Row

E, Graves 5 and 4 respectively. Sons of Adele Denis of Montreal, they were killed on the same day, September 24th, 1917.

Lieutenant Edwin Abbey, 4th CMR, is buried in Plot IV, Row E, Grave 9. Abbey was from Philadelphia, and enlisted in 1915. A book of his letters entitled *An American Soldier* was published posthumously in 1918.

BOIS CARRE BRITISH CEMETERY, Thelus

Thélus is six km north of Arras. The cemetery lies one km east of the village. Plot I was made in April 1917 by the Canadian Corps. After the war another 425 graves were brought in by clearances from the surrounding Vimy battlefield. Although it was initially a 2nd Division burial ground it now contains men from all four Divisions including; 40 - 4th Division killed near Broadmarsh Crater, 70 of the 3rd Division (mostly RCR and PPCLI), 25 - 2nd Division and 87 men from the 1st Division (primarily the 1st (Western Ontario), 3rd (Toronto) and 4th (Central Ontario) Battalions). Five men of the Canadian Light Horse, killed April 9th, 1917, during the cavalry's attempt to breakthrough at Farbus are also buried here.

There are also many burials from later actions when the Canadian Corps was fighting out on the Douai Plain.

In total Bois Carre contains the graves of 500 Commonwealth soldiers, 382 of them Canadian (44 Canadians are unidentified).

The Memorial erected by the 1st Canadian Division in December, 1917 is 200 metres due east of the cemetery.

LA CHAUDIERE MILITARY CEMETERY

La Chaudière Cemetery is located in a hamlet east of Vimy Ridge. The cemetery can be reached by following the main Arras-Lens road to Vimy and then taking the side road to Eleu dit Leauvette (known as Suicide Valley during the war). The cemetery was made next to a German gun position (the bunkers are still there) in April 1917 by the Canadian Corps. After the war many small Canadian cemeteries were concentrated into the cemetery.

La Chaudière Cemetery now contains 917 Commonwealth graves. Of the 638 Canadian burials, 132 are unidentified. The burials in the cemetery represent the Battle of Vimy Ridge with more than 200 graves (predominantly Royal Canadian Regiment) and the heavy fighting at Avion, Liévin and Lens that followed the capture of Vimy Ridge.

Orchard Dump Cemetery, circa 1928.

La Chaudiere Military Cemetery, circa 1928.

Among the graves is that of Private George Pattison, VC, of the 50th Battalion (Alberta). Pattison won his Victoria Cross for bravery near Hill 145 on April 10th, 1917. Pattison's entire machine gun crew was killed on June 3rd, 1917 during the heavy fighting for the electrical generating station near Eleu two km distant. He is buried in Plot VI, Row C, Grave 14, amongst the graves of 22 of his comrades. He was 42.

From the back of the cemetery you can get a excellent view of the Vimy Memorial.

LIEVIN COMMUNAL CEMETERY EXTENSION

The cemetery is located in the southwest side of the old mining town of Lievin, 3 km west of Lens. The cemetery was made after the war by the concentration of ten small cemeteries from the old Vimy-Lens battlefield. It now contains 676 Commonwealth graves, including 153 Canadians (56 are unidentified).

Forty of the Canadian burials are those of men killed in the Battle of Vimy Ridge, and 40 are those killed in the fighting in Lens in August 1917. Half the Vimy graves are men from the 3rd Division killed in La Folie Wood (14 are PPCLI).

ORCHARD DUMP CEMETERY, Arleux-en-Gohelle

Arleux is a village 10 km northeast of Arras. The cemetery is located 2 km southwest of the village. It was started in April 1917 and expanded after the war by 2,900 graves brought in by the clearances of the Arleux-Gravelle-Oppy battlefields.

It now contains 3,005 Commonwealth burials (2,206 unidentified), including 328 Canadians (173 are unidentified). The burials reflect the brutal fighting near Gravelle by the 63rd (Royal Naval) Division, and the failure to exploit the opening success of the Arras Offensive around Oppy in late April 1917.

More than 200 of the Canadian burials belong to men killed in the attacks on the Arleux Loop and Fresnoy in late April and early May 1917.

Amongst those buried here is Lieutenant Clifford A. Wells of the 8th (Little Black Devils) Battalion. Wells was a junior officer from a well-to-do family whose short experience of war was told in a posthumous collection of his letters entitled *From Montreal to Vimy Ridge and Beyond*. He was killed in his first major action, April 28th, 1917 at Arleux. Clifford Wells is buried in Plot IX, Row J, Grave 1.

LICHFIELD CRATER, Thelus (C.B.2A)

The cemetery is in open ground between the villages of Thélus and Neuville-St. Vaast and directly east of the Toll (peage) Motorway. It can be accessed through Neuville-St.Vaast village.

Lichfield Crater Cemetery was made after the battle when the remains of 56 soldiers were buried in a mine crater in what had been No Man's Land. Later the crater was truncated and landscaped. It is one of only two cemeteries in France constructed this way.

The cemetery now contains 52 Canadian graves (of which 10 are unknown), five complete unknowns (probably Canadians) and that of an unknown Russian. A British soldier killed in 1916, whose remains were found during construction, is buried at the edge of the crater.

The names of the 42 known Canadians buried in the crater are engraved on the base of the Cross of Sacrifice. The dead belong to the 2nd Canadian Division; 19th (Central Ontario), 21st (Eastern Ontario) and the 24th (Quebec) Battalions.

Among the dead is Lance Sergeant Ellis Sifton, VC, of the 18th (Western Ontario) Battalion. Sifton was awarded his Victoria Cross posthumously for bravery on April 9th, 1917, when he single-handedly captured an enemy machine gun position and held back a German patrol. He was killed in the final attack.

Thelus Military Cemetery is visible in the open fields to the east.

Grave of the 2nd Canadian Division men killed on Vimy Ridge, July 1918. (Lichfield Crater) Note the Arras-Souchez Road and Notre-Dame de Lorette in the background.

ZIVY CRATER, Thelus (C.B.1)

The cemetery is west of Thélus on the road to Neuville-St. Vaast, immediately west of the Peage Motorway. Its history is similar to that of Lichfield Crater and it contains the graves of 53 Commonwealth soldiers of which 50 are Canadian, two unidentified.

The burials are predominantly men of the 2nd Canadian Division; 18th (Western Ontario), 19th (Central Ontario), 20th (Central Ontario) and 21st (Eastern Ontario) Battalions. The names of the dead are engraved on the base of the Cross of Sacrifice.

You can see Zivy Crater Cemetery from this site.

GIVENCHY ROAD CANADIAN CEMETERY, Neuville-St.Vaast (C.D.1)

The cemetery is found in the Vimy Memorial Park. It was made by the Canadian Corps in April 1917, and contains the graves of 111 Canadian soldiers, one of whom is unidentified. Most burials are 4th Canadian Division, particularly the 102nd (55 burials) and 54th (34 burials) Battalions from British Columbia who were killed on the morning of April 9th, between the cemetery and Broadmarsh Crater.

CANADIAN CEMETERY NO. 2, Neuville-St.Vaast

This Vimy Memorial Park cemetery was established by the Canadian Corps in April 1917. The original burials of Plot I are men from the 4th Division, particularly the 75th Battalion (Mississauga Horse) and the 87th (Grenadier Guards of Montreal) killed in their futile attack on the German trenches defending Hill 145 on April 9th, 1917.

After the war battlefield clearances over a wide area significantly increased the size of the cemetery. It was used as an "Open Cemetery" throughout the 1920s and 30s and received its last Canadian burial in 1947.

The cemetery now contains the graves of 2,966 (72% unidentified) Commonwealth soldiers of which 693 are Canadian (226 unidentified).

Most of the Canadians buried here are from battalions of the 4th Division; 75th (101 identified), 87th (104 identified), 54th (32 identified), 102nd (25 identified), 44th (41 identified), and the 50th (27 identified) Battalions.

The Canadian remains found and re-buried here came from as far away as the Somme (two soldiers found in Regina Trench), but most are from the battlefields near Avion and Lens.

Notre-Dame de Lorette French National Memorial is visible from the northern end of the cemetery.

CABARET ROUGE BRITISH CEMETERY, Souchez

Cabaret Rouge is one km south of Souchez on the main Arras-Béthune road. Souchez is 11 km north of Arras. The cemetery was established in 1916 and used until the end of the war. The original burials are in Plots I through V (the plots far right of the Stone of Remembrance). Battlefield clearances between 1922 and 1927 brought in more than 7,000 burials from areas as far south as Amiens and as far north as Armentières on the Belgian border. It now contains the graves of 7,645 Commonwealth soldiers (59% are unidentified), of which 741 are Canadian (422 are unidentified).

Many are men of the 3rd and 4th Canadian Divisions killed at the Battle of Vimy Ridge are in the plots surrounding the Stone of Remembrance.

The other Canadian burials are related to many battles including Festubert and Givenchy in May and June 1915, the Battle of Hill 70 in August 1917, and the actions near Lens and Avion in May and June 1917. Some men killed in the March 1st, 1917 trench raid are also buried here, most of them unidentified.

This spectacular cemetery contains burials that trace the history of the British Expeditionary Force on the Western Front, 1914-1918. There are many graves of regular British and Indian Army men killed during the Race to the Sea in 1914, the Battles of Neuve Chapelle and Aubers Ridge in 1915, Vimy Ridge in 1916-17 and the Battle of the Lys in 1918. There are also numerous Royal Flying Corps pilots who were killed behind the German lines and whose remains were brought here after the war.

Of interest are the graves of two brothers. Buried in Plot XII, Row E, Graves 16 and 15, Privates Olivier and Wilfred Chenier of the Royal Canadian Regiment, sons of Janvier Olivier, were killed on the same day, April 9th, 1917. They were aged 27 and 28 respectively.

Lieutenant Frederick G. Scott, Canadian Field Artillery, is buried in Plot XV, Row M, Grave19. Scott was a good friend of Conn Smythe, founder of the Toronto Maple Leafs. His sad death had an enormous influence on Smythe and was recounted in his autobiography, *If You Can't Beat 'Em in the Alley.*

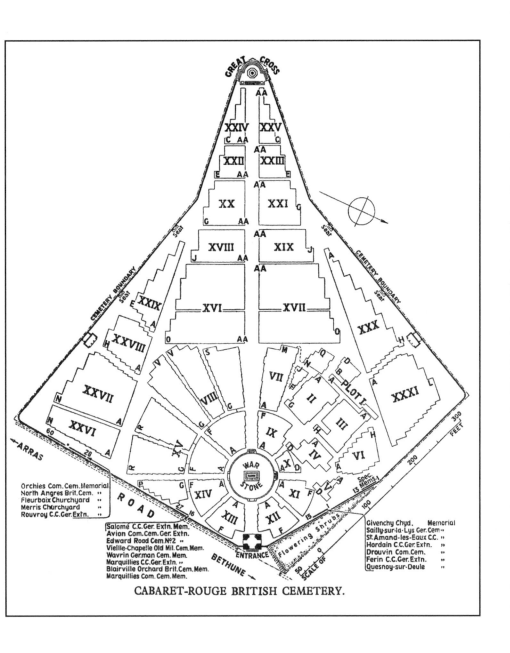

CABARET-ROUGE BRITISH CEMETERY.

In May 2000 the Canadian Government exhumed an Unknown Canadian Soldier and repatriated him to Canada, where he was re-interred as Canada's Unknown Soldier in Ottawa. The body was taken from Plot VIII, Row E, Grave 7. During the battlefield clearances a trench burial containing more than 20 members of the 87th (Canadian Grenadier Guards) Battalion, all killed on the morning of April 9th, 1917, was moved to Cabaret Rouge. Canada's Unknown soldier is one of these men. His identity cannot be confirmed but he is one of 20 or so 87th men who have no known grave and are commemorated on the Vimy Memorial. In place of his old headstone a commemorative marker has been erected. It states:

> THE FORMER GRAVE OF AN
> UNKNOWN CANADIAN SOLDIER
> OF THE FIRST WORLD WAR.
> HIS REMAINS WERE REMOVED
> ON 29 MAY 2000 AND NOW
> LIE INTERRED AT THE
> NATIONAL WAR MEMORIAL
> IN OTTAWA, CANADA.

From the northern side of the cemetery there is an excellent view of the Notre-Dame de Lorette French National Memorial.

GIVENCHY-EN-GOHELLE CANADIAN CEMETERY,
Souchez

Givenchy-en-Gohelle Canadian Cemetery is on the northern part of Vimy Ridge between the Canadian Monument on Hill 145 and The Pimple.

You can reach it via Souchez (it is east of the village) or you can walk along a track north of the Canadian Monument off the road to Givenchy. Made amid the German trenches by the Canadian Corps in April 1917, the cemetery contains the graves of 167 Commonwealth soldiers of which 144 are Canadian (26 unidentified).

The burials in the cemetery are predominantly men of the 4th Division killed April 9th-12th, 1917. Some were killed in the disastrous trench raid of March 1st, 1917. The 72nd (Seaforth Highlanders of Vancouver), 78th (Winnipeg Grenadiers) and the 38th (Eastern Ontario) Battalions all have many burials in this cemetery.

From the cemetery there is a clear view of "The Pimple".

ZOUAVE VALLEY CEMETERY, Souchez

Zouave Valley Cemetery is located in the countryside southeast of Souchez, 11 km north of Arras. The cemetery can be reached through the village, on the same road leading to Givenchy-en-Gohelle Canadian Cemetery. It was established in 1916 and closed in June 1917. After the war battlefield clearances brought in another 42 graves, now buried in Plot I. It contains the graves of 233 Commonwealth soldiers including 93 Canadians, 32 of them unidentified.

Most of the Canadian soldiers buried here were in the 4th Division. Twenty-nine burials are those of men killed on March 1st, 1917 in the failed trench raid. Most served with the 75th Battalion (Mississauga Horse).

ECOIVRES MILITARY CEMETERY, Mont-St.Éloi

Ecoivres Cemetery is one km west of Mont-St-Éloi, west of the main road from Arras to Béthune. The original cemetery was established by the French and used by British and Canadian units between 1916 and 1918. It now contains 1,825 Commonwealth burials including 828 Canadians.

With their headquarters nearby, the 1st, 2nd and 3rd Canadian Divisions used the cemetery throughout 1917. Many units brought back their dead from the front and buried them here. The ruins of Abbe Mont-St-Éloi gave the Canadians a powerful observation post before the Vimy attack. The men who died in the Battle of Vimy Ridge are buried in Plots V and VI.

One of the many tragedies that befell families during the war was the death of father and son, John and Albert Morrison. Driver Albert Morrison of the Canadian Field Artillery, killed on July 5th, 1917, is buried in Plot V, Row K, Grave 11. He was 22. His father, John, was lost when the Luisitania was sunk by a German submarine in 1915.

Private Stanley Tom Stokes of the 1st Battalion (Western Ontario) was killed on April 9th, 1917 at the age of 16. His father, Horace, was killed September 19th, 1917. He was 40. The son is buried in Plot VI, Row E, Grave 3 and his father at Aix-Noulette Communal Cemetery Extension, Plot I, Row T, Grave 2.

Captain Victor Gordon Tupper, MC, grandson of former Prime Minister of Canada Charles Tupper, was killed at Vimy April 9th, 1917 at the age of 21. He is buried in Plot V, Row D, Grave 10.

HE DIED HONOURABLY

April 18th 1917.

Mrs. Kate H. Pegram,
2412 Alder Street,
Vancouver, B. C.
C A N A D A.

Dear Mrs. Pegram;-

It is with the deepest regret that I have to inform you of the death of your son, 129733 Corporal H. A. P. Pegram. He was killed in action during the course of an advance against the Enemy's trenches on April 9th 1917.

Your son was one of the first men to join the Battalion in Vancouver, and his work right up to the time of his death was of an exceedingly high order. Lately he had specialised as a Scout, and in this capacity had done valuable work for me. He had that priceless gift of always being cheerful and seemed to delight in helping his comrades. I cannot tell you how much we all miss him.

It may be some comfort to you to know that your son suffered no pain, as he was killed instantly. I trust that you will accept the sincere sympathy of myself and all ranks of this Battalion in the great loss which you have sustained.

Yours sincerely,

Lieut. Colonel.
72nd Battalion, Canadian Infantry.

Thousands of mothers in countries all over the globe received letters just like this one. Here, the Commanding Officer of the 72nd Battalion (Seaforth Highlanders of Vancouver) tells, in typical fashion, how "cheerful" the young soldier was and how much he will be missed. In the majority of cases, "the letter" would also say that "he died instantly and suffered no pain." It was the kindest thing to say to soothe the fractured emotions of family and there can be no doubt that many did die in this fashion. But many did not.

Henry Pegram was born in Kamloops on January 25, 1895, the only son of Kate Pegram of Vancouver. He enlisted in 1915 in the 72nd Battalion at Vancouver where he worked as a warehouseman.

In May 1916, he was shipped overseas with the 72nd Battalion. He was promoted to Corporal and fought on the Somme in October and November of 1916. At the age of 22, Pegram was killed in the warren of trenches near Montreal Crater captured by the 72nd on April 9, 1917. He is buried in Givenchy-en-Gohelle Canadian Cemetery on the Ridge.

The headstone commemorating Private Henry Pegram, 72nd Battalion (Seaforth Highlanders), killed in action April 9, 1917. The personal inscription reads:

> *Greater love*
> *hath no man*
> *than he who giveth*
> *his life for another.*

There are two sets of Canadian brothers buried in Ecoivres. Henry and Walter Crossley, both of the 27th (City of Winnipeg) Battalion are buried in Plot IV, Row K, Graves 12 and 13. Henry was killed at Vimy Ridge on March 29th, 1917 and Walter was killed two days later. They were the sons of James and Elizabeth Crossley of Winnipeg, Manitoba.

Dave and Charlie Meteer, of St. Thomas, Ontario were killed at Vimy Ridge only two weeks apart, April 1st and April 15th, 1917 respectively. They are buried in Plot V, Row A, Grave 1 and Plot VI, Row E, Grave 28.

VILLERS STATION CEMETERY, Viller-au-Bois

Villers-au-Bois is 10 km north of Arras. Two km north of the vilage, off the road to Gouy-Servins, is Villers Station cemetery. This cemetery was established by the French in 1914 and used by British and Canadian units between 1916 and 1918. The French graves were later removed to their national cemetery at Notre-Dame de Lorette. It contains the graves of 1,207 Commonwealth soldiers of which 1,009 are Canadian (one unidentified).

Many graves are soldiers of the 4th Division, whose headquarters were at the Chateau de la Haie, across the road from the cemetery. The burials related to the Battle of Vimy Ridge are in Plots V through X. The cemetery is a record of Canada's history on the Vimy Front. The burials date from October 1916 into the summer of 1918.

Amongst the burials is Major Frank Sare, 87th Battalion killed at Vimy April 9th, 1917. His sister, Gladys Irene Sare was a Canadian Nursing Sister. She was one of 14 nurses who perished when a Hospital Ship, HMHS Llandovery Castle, was sunk by a German U-Boat in 1918. Miss Sare has no known grave and is commemorated on the Halifax Memorial.

Brothers Donald and George Neale were both killed with the 46th (Saskatchewan) Battalion. Donald died June 20th, 1917 and George was killed on April 13th, 1917. They are buried in Plot VIII, Row D, Grave 14 and Plot VIII, Row A, Grave 5. They were the sons of Henry and May Jane Neale of Cater, Saskatchewan.

The Commanding Officers of both the 75th (Mississauga Horse) and the 54th (Kootenay, British Columbia) Battalions, Lieutenant Colonel Samuel Gustavus Beckett (Plot VII, Row D, Grave 1) of Toronto and Lieutenant Colonel Arnold Kemball, CB, DSO, (Plot VI, Row E, Grave 1) of Kaslo, British Columbia are buried here. They were both killed in the disastrous trench raid during the Battle of Vimy Ridge on March 1st, 1917. Kemball was 56. Many of the officers and men killed in the raid are buried close by.

Captain Hugh Pedley, MC, Canadian Light Trench Mortar Battery, was killed at Lens on January 31st, 1918. He was the cousin of Lieutenant James H. Pedley, MC, 4th (Central Ontario) Battalion. In his memoir, *Only This*, J.H. Pedley recounts visiting his cousin's grave in 1918, when he was stationed in the Canadian Camp on the grounds of Chateau de la Haie. He is buried in Plot XI, Row B, Grave 21.

Probably the saddest grave in the cemetery is that of Victor Tallis. He was one of four brothers killed in the war, all serving with the 46th Battalion. Victor was killed at Vimy on February 19th, 1917, Arnold was killed at the Drocourt-Queant line on September 2nd, 1918, Harold was killed at Valenciennes on November 1st, 1918 and Edgar died of wounds received at Ypres on September 11th, 1916. Two other Tallis family members from Borden, Saskatchewan, William and Sydney, survived the war. All six enlisted in the 65th Battalion. Victor Tallis is buried in Plot VII, Row B, Grave 22.

QUATRE VENTS MILITARY CEMETERY, Estree-Cauchy

Quatre Vents Cemetery, directly east of the main road from Arras to Bruay, was established by the French in 1915 and used by Canadian and British Field Ambulances and fighting units between 1916 and 1918. The graves of 132 Commonwealth soldiers now lie there. Seventy-seven of them are Canadian.

The cemetery contains 53 men who died in the Battle of Vimy Ridge (mostly 1st Division). Two of the 25 Canadian soldiers executed during the war, Private H. Kerr of the 7th Battalion (British Columbia) was executed November 21st, 1916 for desertion. Private John Higgins of the 1st Battalion (Western Ontario) was executed for desertion December 7th, 1916. He was 24. They are buried in Plot III, Row A, Grave 9 and Plot I, Row B, Grave 2.*

---

* Ecoivres and Villers Station also contain the graves of Canadians executed.

Many war graves have a few lines engraved near the base of each headstone. These epitaphs, known as Private or Personal Inscriptions, were provided to the Imperial (later Commonwealth) War Graves Commission by the families of the Fallen in the 1920s. It not uncommon to find them in Hebrew, French, Latin, Greek, Afrikaans or in the case of Private Victor Sorenson, in Danish. Sorenson (III.A.8) was killed at Vimy Ridge, April 9th, 1917, serving with the 10th (Alberta) Battalion.

The regions north and west of Vimy Ridge are riddled with cemeteries that contain hundreds of Canadian graves. Although those listed below do not contain many Battle of Vimy Ridge burials, they do reflect the immense sacrifice made by the Canadians during their time on the Vimy front. These other cemeteries are: BEEHIVE CEMETERY, Willerval, BOIS-DE-NOULETTE BRITISH CEMETERY, TRANCHEE DES MECKNES CEMETERY, AIX-NOULETTE COMMUNAL CEME-TERY EXTENSION, VIMY COMMUNAL CEMETERY, PETIT VIMY BRITISH CEMETERY, LA TARGETTE BRITISH CEME-TERY, SUCRERIE CEMETERY, LOUEZ BRITISH CEMETERY and ANZIN-ST.AUBIN BRITISH CEMETERY.

THE HOSPITAL CEMETERIES

The wounded were evacuated quickly from the battlefield and taken by field ambulance or light gauge railway to the Casualty Clearing Stations for immediate treatment. Those with femur or abdominal wounds and those with head injuries who had little hope of survival would remain at the Casualty Clearing Station. The others would be transported, usually by train, to the main hospital centres on the Channel coast.

BARLIN COMMUNAL CEMETERY EXTENSION

The cemetery is north of the village of Barlin, which is north of the Lens-Béthune road and 10 km east of Béthune. The cemetery was estab-lished by the French in 1914 and subsequently taken over by British and Canadian Casualty Clearing Stations.

It now contains the graves of 1,095 Commonwealth soldiers includ-ing 677 Canadians. More than 200 burials are Canadians mortally wounded in the capture of Vimy Ridge. Many of the others died of wounds received holding the line in front of Vimy or on the Douai Plain later in the year. Fifty graves belong to men who died of wounds received during the Battle of Hill 70 in August 1917.

Buried in Plot I, Row J, Grave 50 is Lieutenant Alfred Norsworthy of the 73rd Battalion (Black Watch of Montreal). Norsworthy died of wounds March 29th, 1917. His older brother, Major Edward Norsworthy, was killed while on active service with the 13th Battalion (Black Watch of Montreal). On April 22nd, 1915, Major Norsworthy's courageous action against the Germans on the Canadian's open flank helped save the day during the poison gas attack (see For King & Empire;Volume I; The Canadians at Ypres, April, 1915).

Company Quarter Master Sergeant William Alexander has the unfortunate claim of being the highest ranking Canadian executed during the war. Alexander had served at the front since February 1915 without running afoul of the military authorities. He deserted during the Battle of Hill 70, and was recaptured shortly after and tried for Desertion. In spite of his clean record nothing could not save him from the firing squad, including a last-minute effort by the Chaplain of the 1st Canadian Division, Frederick Scott. The highly-respected Padre appealed to Alexander's Commanders but to no avail. He was shot on October 18th, 1917. His case was one of the most tragic of the war as it seemed so blatantly unfair. Canon Scott wrote of that awful night in his memoir *The Great War As I Saw It* (CEF Books, 2000).

His family in Winnipeg was torn apart by his shocking death and wrote; "May the Lord have Mercy on the man who judged him, if he was wrong." CQMS Alexander is buried in Plot II, Row D, Grave 43.

LAPUGNOY MILITARY CEMETERY

The cemetery is northwest of the village of Lapugnoy (six km west of Béthune). It was established in 1915 and used for burials from nearby Casualty Clearing Stations. It now contains 1,319 Commonwealth graves (including more than 150 British soldiers killed in the Battle of Loos, September 1915), 349 of them are Canadian (one unknown).

One hundred and thirty-three of the Canadians buried here were wounded in the Battles of Vimy Ridge, Arleux and Fresnoy. Another 49 succumbed to their wounds received in the Battle of Hill 70. Canadian units also buried their dead here in 1918. Lapugnoy was central to much of the Canadian operations on the Vimy front for 18 months.

Victor Wheeler, a Signaller in the 50th (Alberta) Battalion, wrote a powerful memoir of his experiences on the Western Front. Wheeler's heart-felt memoir, *The 50th Battalion in No Man's Land* (CEF Books, 2000), recounts life with his closest friends, the Waller brothers, Art, Harry and Robert of Calgary, Alberta. During the attack on the Pimple, Harry was severely wounded by an explosion when entering a German dugout. Barely alive and almost cut in two, Harry rested in his brother Art's arms, until he was stretchered away. He died 5 days later. Art was killed a year later. Robert survived the war. Harry Waller is buried in Plot III, Row A, Grave 13.

BRUAY COMMUNAL CEMETERY EXTENSION

The cemetery is located northwest of the old coal mining village of Bruay, which is five km west of Béthune. Set amongst the monumental slag heaps, it was established by French troops in October 1914 and used by British and Canadian units from 1916 to 1918. It contains the graves of 412 Commonwealth soldiers of which 276 are Canadian.

Sixty-three of the Canadian burials belong to those who died of wounds received in the Battle of Vimy Ridge. The rest of the Canadian graves are those mortally wounded while holding the line through 1917 or in the Battle of Hill 70 (24).

ETAPLES MILITARY CEMETERY

Etaples Cemetery is on the coastal road between Boulogne and Le Touquet, three km north of the village of Etaples (100 km west of Arras). Etaples was a major base for the British army on the Western Front and was the location of the infamous Bull Ring and the British mutiny of 1917. The cemetery was used throughout the war and contains 10,729 Commonwealth graves, including 1,123 Canadians. It is the second largest CWGC cemetery in France, second only to St. Sever Communal Cemetery and Extension in Rouen.

This cemetery reflects the Canadian losses during the major actions of Mount Sorrel, the Somme, Vimy, Passchendaele and the Advance to Victory. More than 100 graves belong to Canadians who succumbed to wounds received at Vimy Ridge.

On May 19th, 1918, German Gotha bombers made direct hits on the No.1 Canadian General Hospital, killing 66 people, including three nursing sisters. The men killed in the attack are buried in Plots LXVI, LXVII and LXVIII. The nursing sisters are buried in Plot XXVIII.

BOULOGNE EASTERN CEMETERY, FRANCE

Boulogne is 100 km west of Arras on the English Channel coast. The cemetery, in the eastern part of the city, was used from 1914 to 1918 and contains 442 Canadian burials. Due to soil conditions, the headstones lie flat. A hospital centre throughout the war, Boulogne is typical of many hospital centre cemeteries. The officers are separated from the other ranks, the men are buried in chronological order, three to a grave here, and there are few unknowns.*

The Canadians buried here died of wounds received in every Canadian action 1915-1917. There are fifty men buried here who died of wounds received in the Second Battle Ypres, 1915, 57 from the Battle of the Somme, 54 from Mount Sorrel and 109 who died as a result of wounds received in the Battle of Vimy Ridge.

Of interest is the grave of Lieutenant Frederick W. Campbell, VC, of the 1st Canadian Battalion (Western Ontario). Campbell won his Victoria Cross for bravery in the Battle of Givenchy in June 1915. He was severely wounded in the action and died four days later.

Alwyn Bramley-Moore, Princess Patricia's Canadian Light Infantry, is buried in Plot VIII, Row D, Grave 91. A transplanted Englishman, Bramley-Moore wrote of his wartime life in letters to his family, later published in a book entitled *The Path Of Duty*. His war cut short when he was mortally wounded by a sniper on the Ypres front, March 28th, 1916. He died on April 4th.

WIMEREUX COMMUNAL CEMETERY

The cemetery is located in the village of Wimereux, which is seven km north of Boulogne, on the channel coast. The cemetery was used by hospitals from 1915 until filled in 1918.

It contains the graves of 2,847 Commonwealth soldiers of which 216 are Canadian. Due to ground instability all the first World War headstones are recumbent. Seventy-one of the Canadian burials are soldiers who died of wounds received at Vimy Ridge. There are also Canadian graves from the Battles of Ypres, 1915 (23), Festubert (12), the Somme (16), Mount Sorrel (10) and Passchendaele (16).

Perhaps the most famous Canadian to die in the Great War is buried at Wimereux. Lieutenant-Colonel John McCrae, Canadian Army

---

* It also contains several plots of graves of Second World War serviceman and a plot of Portuguese burials from the First World War.

Medical Corps, who died of pneumonia while on active service January 28th, 1918, is buried in the officers' section, Plot IV, Row H, Grave 3. His poem *In Flanders Fields* is one of the longest lasting symbols of the First World War. Almost 90 years have passed since he wrote it in a dressing station during the Second Battle of Ypres, yet it still has the power to move even the most idle listener. At the entrance of the cemetery is a memorial plaque and bench dedicated to Colonel McCrae.

NEUVILLE-ST. VAAST GERMAN CEMETERY

I have always found the German cemeteries in France eerie and uncomfortable. With their black metal crosses and lack of flowers, these stark, dark burial grounds carry an atmosphere of sadness and reflect the malignancy of war.

There are 214 German cemeteries in France, representing both world wars. The Neuville-St. Vaast German Cemetery in the Vimy area is the largest cemetery in the region. Built over the German battle position known as The Labyrinthe, captured by the French in 1915 after heavy fighting, it contains 44,833 burials at last count. Remains are still being found on a regular basis.

Uniquely German, this huge cemetery reflects the standard design of most German cemeteries. A black metal cross marks four graves, while the headstone-type memorials signify graves of Jewish soldiers.

Similar to the French cemeteries, the German ones often contain a mass grave. In Neuville-St. Vaast, the mass burial site runs along the northern perimeter and contains some 8,000 bodies.

In addition to the German cemeteries, thousands of German soldiers are buried in Commonwealth cemeteries where for the most part, they died as prisoners-of-war.

The cemetery is located 1 km south of Neuville-St. Vaast, on the road to Arras.

ALLWARD'S DREAM

The idea for the magnificent Canadian National Monument, which sits majestically on the Vimy Ridge, came to Toronto architect and sculptor Walter S. Allward in a dream.

Overlooking the Douai Plain on the ridge captured by the Canadian Corps on April 9th, 1917, the monument commemorates the 60,000 Canadians who gave their lives in the Great War.

Allward's design won the 1921 National Memorial competition and work began in France in 1925. The project went slowly as workers had to cope with a warren of tunnels, mine craters, shell holes, trenches and dugouts on the old Vimy battlefield. The massive number of unexploded shells of all calibers and live grenades prevented the use of large earthmoving equipment. Each section of the construction site had to be cleared by pick and shovel and many men were injured.

It took two years to complete the 3.5 kilometre road leading from Thélus to the monument on Hill 145. Before construction of the road began, craters were drained and rammed and more than 26 dugouts filled and concreted over. Evidence of uncharted dugouts appeared when the ground subsided following heavy rains.

Similar work was required to build the foundation of the monument. More than 15,000 tonnes of concrete and steel reinforcing bars were used to build it. Two men were killed in this phase of the operation.

The next step was the construction of the bastion, the symbol of impregnable defence, surmounted by two pylons representing the gate to eternity and the two countries that paid so heavily to capture the ridge.

The final phase was the sculpting of the 20 statues Allward had envisaged. Each represents a virtue, a higher ideal achieved by the sacrifice of the Canadians. Each statue was sculpted in situ, with a special studio constructed for each. Half-sized plaster models were used by the sculptors. Six thousand tonnes of Trau limestone, quarried from the Dalmatian coast, was used for the monument.

The memorial was unveiled on July 26th, 1936 by King Edward VIII in the presence of thousands of Canadian veterans and war widows who made the pilgrimage to pay homage to their fallen comrades.

On approaching the memorial, the first statues viewed are the reclining man on the right and a woman on the left, the mourners reflecting on the grief felt by many Canadian families. Angels, carved toward the top of the pylons, guard the gate. This is the "back" of the memorial.

The tomb of Canada's fallen – The Vimy Memorial
(PHOTO: N. CHRISTIE)

At the front of the monument, between the pylons, are two figures representing the spirit of sacrifice and the passing of the torch. They gaze upwards toward the celestial values.

The three statues on the left pylon reflect Truth and Faith, surmounted by Justice. On the right pylons, similarly represented, are Charity and Knowledge, surmounted by Peace. These spiritual figures are chanting the hymn of peace. The main statue facing the Douai Plain represents the Spirit of Canada mourning her fallen sons. This figure is the largest of the 20 statues and was sculpted from a single 30-tonne block of Dalmatian limestone. At the base of the right-hand stairs of the monument is a group of three statues illustrating the breaking of the sword and the defiance and defeat of militarism. In the centre of the bastion is the tomb of the fallen Canadian soldier, representing all those who died. The last group of four statues at the base of the left-hand stairs, represents Canada defending the helpless.

Engraved on the walls of the monument are the names of the 11,285 Canadian soldiers who died in France but were denied a known grave by the fortunes of war. They are listed alphabetically and, secondarily, by rank. The graves of more than 100 men have been found since the panels were engraved in the 1930s.

Vimy under construction

Walter Allward at Vimy

Vimy under construction

(PUBLIC ARCHIVES OF CANADA)

Vimy under construction

(PUBLIC ARCHIVES OF CANADA)

More than 20 sets of brothers, a father and his son and a Count are named on the memorial. Each name has its own sad story. For example, Private Harold Chapman served as a Major with British forces in Gallipoli in 1915, was wounded and discharged. He returned to Canada and reenlisted in Vancouver. He was killed at Hill 70 August 15th, 1917.

There are four Victoria Cross winners commemorated on the memorial. They are Private William Johnstone Milne, who won his VC posthumously on April 9th, 1917; Lieutenant Robert Grierson Combe, killed at Fresnoy May 3rd, 1917; Sergeant Frederick Hobson, who won his VC posthumously at Lens in August 1917; and Sergeant Robert Spall, who won his VC posthumously at Parvillers on August 13th, 1918.

There is also at least one man listed who did not die. Private McDonald was listed as wounded and missing in 1918. His pension was paid to his widow and the case was closed until 1957 when another wife of Private McDonald reported his death to local authorities. He had married in England for a second time in 1917, deserted in 1918, returned to Canada and lived the last 40 years of his life in British Columbia!

The memorial is surrounded by 100 hectares (250 acres) of the Vimy battleground, a gift in perpetuity from France to Canada. Within the park, trenches have been preserved along the "crater line" and tours of the underground tunnels are available from April to November.

Dedication Inscription - The Vimy Memorial

(PHOTO; N. CHRISTIE)

Unveiling Ceremony of the

CANADIAN NATIONAL MONUMENT

AT

VIMY RIDGE

JULY 26th, 1936

3 Days ——————— £7

VIMY. ABOUT 1920.

or INCLUDING

PARIS AND VERSAILLES

7 Days ——————— £13

London—back to London.

THE VIMY PILGRIMAGE, JULY, 1936

Nineteen years after the Battle of Vimy Ridge, more than 6,000 Canadian pilgrims set sail for Europe. They joined a crowd of an estimated 100,000 people gathered in northern France to witness the dramatic unveiling of the Canadian National Memorial on July 26th, 1936. This was the day Canada would remember her dead.

It was one of the first large reunions since The Great War. For several years after the war ended, few surviving veterans indulged in reminiscence. The occasional soldier, widow and mother returned to northern France to search for the graves of their fallen loved ones, but the event was too recent to allow any feelings of nostalgia.

Mourning faded by the end of the 1920s, however, and dozens of books about the war were published and sold to the seemingly insatiable public.

The first great Canadian Corps Reunion was held in Toronto in 1934. Former combatants, many now in their forties, began to experience a need to reaffirm their loyalty to their comrades. Although these were the Depression years, the camaraderie of those who served in the Canadian Corps brought together more than 50,000 veterans for the three-day celebration, the services and the banquets. Memories were shared, reminiscences retold.

A French village, complete with manure pile, was constructed in the west wing of the Coliseum! And a tattoo was performed in honour of the Canadian Corps' famous leader, Sir Arthur Currie, who had died the previous year.

It was the Canadian Legion who conceived the Vimy pilgrimage to the battlefields of the First World War to coincide with the unveiling of Canada's National Memorial on Vimy Ridge, scheduled for completion in 1936. The response from the Legion's membership was phenomenal. More than 7,500 people responded. The cost for the trip from Montreal to Vimy was $160 and included a beret, armband and guide.

On July 16th, 1936, 6,200 Canadian pilgrims boarded five ocean liners and set off across the Atlantic. The Canadian Legion had organized an itinerary for each ship, arranged hotels, port visits, and meals. Another 1,500 Canadian veterans, living in the United Kingdom, joined up with the pilgrimage in France. Everyone would meet at Vimy on July 26th, 1936.

Aerial view of the Canadian National Memorial, Vimy Ridge, July 26, 1936.
(PUBLIC ARCHIVES OF CANADA)

H. M. King Edward VIII unveiling the figure of Canada, July 26, 1936
(PUBLIC ARCHIVES OF CANADA)

Unlike that cold, wet and miserable Easter Monday so many years ago, the unveiling ceremony took place under sunny skies. There were some 100,000 people gathered at the Canadian Memorial. Lines of French soldiers, mounted Moroccan Saphis, and flights of aircraft created a sense of drama to the event.

Dignitaries such as Vincent Massey, the Canadian High Commissioner for London, were there as well as two of his underlings, George Vanier and Lester Pearson. So were former generals of the Canadian Corps, Turner VC, MacDonnell, and Burstall and the widows of the two successful commanders of the Corps, Lady Currie and Lady Byng.* The government of France was also represented by many dignitaries. It was a grand occasion.

The crowd cheered the arrival of King Edward VIII. During the war, he had often accompanied the Canadians at the front and he was immensely popular with them.

The King's appearance was the signal for the band to start up the national anthem**, followed by "O Canada." He then inspected the Guards of Honour, including the Veterans Guard composed of ex-CEF soldiers.

Before taking his place opposite the sheathed statue of the Spirit of Canada, the King mingled with the veterans and the war widows, who were given a place of honour at the front of the Canadian pilgrims.

Honorary Lieut.-Colonel the Reverend C.C. Owen of Vancouver opened the service. "...Memories crowd back as we tread the ground again and we think of the lessons learned, or which should have been learned — by a war-weary world," he said.

After the memorial services given by the padres, the King spoke to the hushed crowd. He spoke of the sacrifice of the Canadian Corps and of the French gesture of giving Vimy Ridge to Canada.

"The laws of France have decreed that Canada shall stand forever." He finished his speech on a note of thanks. "In that spirit, in a spirit of thankfulness for their example, of reverence for their devotion and of pride in their comradeship, I unveil this memorial to Canada's dead."

The folds of the Union Jack enveloping the Spirit of Canada fell away and the Last Post sounded, followed by two minutes of silence and then, Reveille.

---

* Lady Byng was immortalized in Canada's heritage when she instituted The Lady Byng Trophy for the most gentlemanly player in the National Hockey League.
** God Save the King.

Fly past at the unveiling of the Vimy Memorial, July 26, 1936.

(PUBLIC ARCHIVES OF CANADA)

French President Lebrun spoke next. He affirmed the sacrifice and Canada's place in history.

"The masterpiece which rises before our eyes," said Lebrun, "by its grandiose dimensions, its proud and pure symbolism, is one of the most remarkable among the many which commemorate on the field of battle the valour and abnegation of warriors."

He continued, "May this monument henceforth dominate with its imposing mass the immense plain which lies before us.

"...It will recall to them that here several hundred thousand men, from a faraway land, spilled their blood to defend their hearth; that they were willing to sacrifice their lives not for the satisfaction of material interests but for the beauty of an ideal and the mobility of a memory; that many of them, faithful to the call of blood, recalling the Champlains, the Maisonneuves and the Cavaliers de la Salle, de Montcalm, returned to their ancient motherland to defend and revivify it by mingling with it again.

"It is a noble and great example," Lebrun said to the crowd. "May this magnificent self-sacrifice not be lost for the lessons of the future. May this memorial, a vigilant sentinel in the centre of the fields still echoing with human grief, teach us that more powerful and more profound than community of race and blood there exists a higher solidarity which should always guide the actions of men."

As President Lebrun finished, so the ceremony closed. The Pilgrims scattered the ashes from wooden crosses and Shields of David which had originally marked the graves of Canadians in France and Flanders. They then swarmed over the memorial in search of the names of lost comrades and brothers amongst the 12,000 listed on the stone base.

As one Canadian pilgrim stated, "Without us, their vision fades."

The 6,000 or so pilgrims then visited Ypres in Belgium and England, where further emotional receptions and ceremonies were held at Westminster and the cenotaph at Whitehall.

On August 1st 5,000 Canadians crossed again to France. For many, this was the most memorable part of the trip. The hospitality and genuine affection shown by their French hosts deeply impressed the Canadians. After a ceremony of the Unknown Soldier at the Arc de Triomphe in Paris and a few more days of touring, the Canadians returned home.

For many of the pilgrims, the opportunity to revisit the battlefields and to assure their fallen comrades that they were "unforgotten dead" relieved some of the sadness left by the war. For mothers who lost sons* and the many widows who came to see the graves of their lost husbands for the one and only time**, the pilgrimage alleviated some of the pain.

Sadly, Vimy claimed another victim. On July 28th Mrs. Rose Anne Kemp of Calgary fell ill during the pilgrimage and died. One of her last acts was to place a wreath on her late husband's grave. (Private Thomas Kemp is buried in Villers Station Cemetery near Vimy. He had been killed June 26th, 1917 at Avion.)

The importance of this Pilgrimage to the men who made the trip cannot be understated. The financial sacrifice for most during the depression years indicated the "need" many had to make the journey.

One of the Vimy Pilgrims was Randall Christie, my grandfather. The Vimy Pilgrimage was probably the greatest highlight of his life. He treasured his memories of Vimy and saved every document, postcard and souvenir, from his special "Vimy Passport", specially issued for the Pilgrims, to food coupons and a 1935 London Underground schedule. It was his one and only chance to revisit "that" past and it stayed with him forever.

The unique Canadian Passport issued for the Vimy Pilgrimage.

---

* The First Silver Cross mother was Mrs. C. S. Wood of Winnipeg who lost five sons in war. One son, Private Peter Percy Wood is commemorated on the Memorial.

** In general, this was the one and only time for most, due to the fact the Commonwealth (then Imperial) War Graves Commision, through government legislation, had blocked repatriation of remains.

This Sun Life of Canada advertisement in The Vimy Pilgrimage Guide 1936 captures the National feeling towards the Pilgrimage.

MINING WARFARE

Mining warfare was not a new tactic in the First World War. Tunnelling under an enemy's position and detonating large explosive charges was used during the American Civil War and in the Russo-Japanese War. This type of warfare was always used against a heavily entrenched, defensive position and never carried a guarantee of success.

The First World War provided entrenched, defensive positions like no other and it was not surprising mining warfare became a significant method of waging war.

After the Race to the Sea in 1914, the front lines stabilized and both sides, particularly the Germans, constructed deep fortified trenches underground with deep dugouts and galleries often 70 metres or more in depth to defend the territory won in 1914. In 1915, both sides were tunnelling furiously all along the Western Front. Near Ypres, Armentières, Vimy, the Chemin de Dames and the Champagne, French and German tunnellers commenced the underground war.

Nowhere on the Western Front was mining more active than on Vimy Ridge. In the First World War thousands of mines were exploded by both sides, but more than 200 mines were blown at Vimy alone.

Today, in Vimy Park, the massive craters are evidence of the severity of the mining. Few craters survive outside the park. The ridge between Givenchy and Souchez villages was once riven with craters. All have been filled in.

When mining started in 1915, the armies looked for men with mining experience, engineers and geologists. Within a few months, full staffs were planning and digging to wrest the underground advantage from the Germans.

In general, a mine shaft would be sunk close behind the front lines. It would gradually decline to a level of 15 to 25 metres, at which point galleries would be pushed out under a German position. In the meantime, the Germans would be doing the same. Each mine would be constructed at a specific level, with a specific size of explosive charge. Usually the explosion of the mine would correspond with an infantry assault, either a major attack or localized action.

Mines were employed offensively and defensively. Offensively, they were utilized to eliminate a strong point, a cement bunker or a weapons emplacement. They were also used less dramatically, for instance, to obtain a better observation post or field of fire.

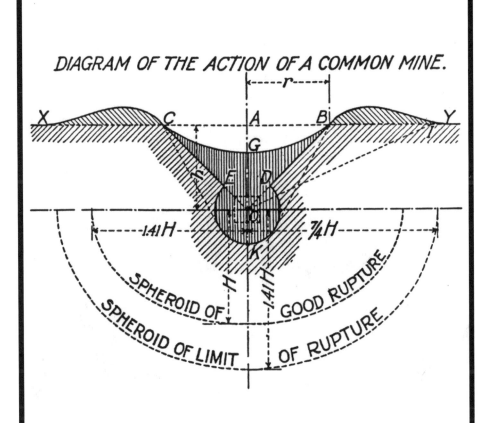

THE IDEAL CRATER

Line of least resistance	(A-O)
Radius of crater	(AB)
Radius of explosion	(OB)
Radius of circle of friability	(AI)
Radius of friability	(OI)
Depth of crater	(AG)
Vertical radius of rupture	(H)

Defensive mining involved trying to undo what your opponents were doing. Vigilance was the key — listening to enemy activity both on the surface and from within the gallery. The "geophone" was the most precise and accurate listening device. Preferably at night, the men would listen for the dragging of bags or boxes (explosives), knocking out of timber supports, signals or any form of activity which might indicate a possible explosion. The Germans would often have two pick men build a chamber in which to place the explosives.* The men would watch for new chalk mounds, fresh earth, sandbags of a different colour, new trenches, mining spoil** and anything that could indicate the shaft of a possible mine.

The defensive objective was to eliminate the enemy shafts by the use of camouflets. Camouflets were mine charges designed to collapse the enemy's galleries. A mine barrage, or series of mines, could collapse a series of parallel galleries or chambers.

Whether the mining was offensive or defensive, many factors had to be taken into consideration. Of vital importance were the nature and contour of the ground, the distance to enemy position (mines were rarely used to attack positions more than 100 metres away), the nature of the strata (chalk or clay) and the water level.

The shafts were usually sunk in the support trenches. At Vimy, the galleries were usually 20-50 metres deep. The gallery would run to the required position underneath the target. A series of chambers would be dug to hold the explosive charges of, usually, ammonal. The explosive chambers would be tamped, that is, the ends of the gallery would be blocked with sandbags, interspersed with spaces. The tamping would protect the gallery and the rest of the mine and ensure the full force of the explosion was vertical.

The complexity of this warfare is hard to grasp. Underneath the crater line at the "preserved trenches," there are at least seven galleries around the Duffield Craters alone! Life for the miners must have been hard and the hazards were great. On more than one occasion, British galleries opened into German galleries and hand-to-hand fighting ensued.

---

* Chalk was a noisy material in which to work. Clay was considerably quieter and enabled the miners to accomplish much before being detected.

** Disposal of spoil was a real problem for both sides especially at Vimy. The chalk spoil was exposed against the surface clay.

But the worst fear must have been felt by the infantry at the strong posts or weapons emplacements in the front lines, when they knew the mining was going on. To avoid creating alarm amongst the infantry, the miners were not allowed to discuss the situation. When a "blow" was anticipated, the Mining Officer would inform the Infantry Officer, who would then withdraw his troops from exposed positions.

No doubt some men would have to remain in these important positions, anticipating the moment they could be blown to smithereens. The optimum time for a "blow" was at "stand-to" at dawn or dusk when the maximum number of enemy troops was in the front line.

The Germans dominated the underground war on Vimy Ridge until a concerted effort by the Royal Engineers altered the balance. The 172nd Tunnelling Company, Royal Engineers, fired as many as four mines a night in mid-1916. This so severely affected the Germans that in May 1916 they launched a localized attack to seize the British mine shafts.

Mining warfare continued throughout 1917, with the largest one-time use of mines in the Battle of Messines, June 1917. Nineteen huge mines devastated the German positions from Messines to Hill 60 near Ypres. Mining warfare petered out after that and the miners were reassigned to other duties.

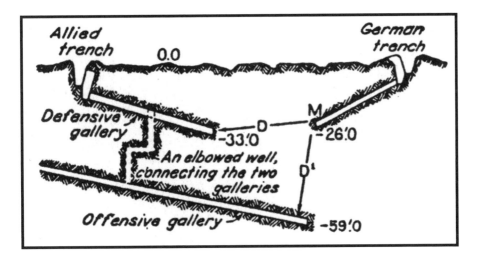

Theoretical Mine Gallery system.

FOR FURTHER REFERENCE

More books have been written on the Battle of Vimy Ridge than on all other Canadian battles combined. There is certainly no shortage of background information on this action. However, only one book has been written on the complete Battle of Arras 1917, including the attacks of the British, Australian and Canadians. Listed below are a number of excellent books on Vimy.

This book has concerned itself solely with the Battle of Vimy Ridge. There is much more to see and explore on the Western Front and I have included in the list below some excellent guides.

BOOKS ON THE BATTLE OF VIMY RIDGE

Vimy, by P. Barton, McClelland and Stewart, 1986.
Vimy Ridge, by A. McKee, Souvenir Press, 1966.
The Shadow of Vimy Ridge, by K. Macksey, Ryerson, 1965.
Vimy!, by H. F. Wood, MacMillan of Canada, 1967.
Cheerful Sacrifice, by G. Nicols, Leo Cooper, 1990.
Canada at Vimy by D.E. Macintyre, Peter Martin, 1967.
Letters of Agar Adamson (ed. N.M. Christie.) CEF Books, 1997.
The Journal of Private Fraser (ed. R.H. Roy) CEF Books, 1998.
The 50TH Battalion in No Man's Land by V.W. Wheeler. CEF Books, 2000.
The Great War As I Saw It by F.G. Scott. CEF Books, 2000.

GUIDEBOOKS TO THE WESTERN FRONT

The Western Front, Then and Now, by J. Giles, Battle of Britain Prints International, 1992.
Before Endeavours Fade, by R. E. Coombs, Battle of Britain Prints International, 1976.
The Somme Battlefields, by M. & M. Middlebrook, Viking 1991.
Australian Battlefields of the Western Front by John Laffin. Kangaroo, 1992
For King & Empire series, Vols I - VIII (Ypres, Somme, Vimy, Passchendaele, Arras, Amiens, Cambrai and Mount Sorrel) by Norm Christie, CEF Books, 1996-2001.